Good Enough for the

Richest

And

Open to the Poorest

Jean Pierce

Teresa A. Wasonga

Good Enough for the Richest and Open to the Poorest

Copyright © 2016 by Jean Pierce and Teresa A. Wasonga

Published by SANGO Publishing

ISBN: 978-0692656600 (soft cover)

Contents

"Good enough for the richest and open to the poorest."

Horace Mann

Prologue

In 2011, Teresa Wasonga and her husband, Andrew Otieno, opened a secondary school for indigent girls in rural Kenya. The school was named Jane Adeny (pronounced uh-DENN) Memorial School in honor of Teresa's mother. The task was accomplished in a country where less than 20% of the population completes secondary school and only three percent receive a university diploma.

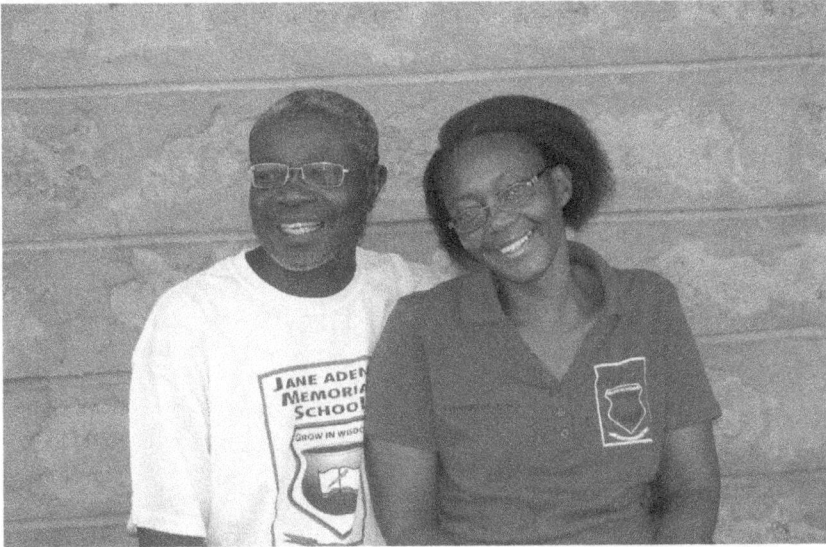

Andrew and Teresa

Each week, over a period of several months, I met with Teresa, and occasionally with Andrew, in a coffee shop in DeKalb, Illinois, where they shared the remarkable stories captured in this book. Teresa is a Professor of Educational Administration, and Andrew is a Professor of Engineering at Northern Illinois University. As a professor of

Educational Psychology, I was one of Teresa's colleagues.

As Teresa spoke about her vision and experiences creating the school, it was clear that she was accomplishing a remarkable feat:

- The school is unique in the region, since it applies the latest learning research
- Impoverished yet talented girls are being given an opportunity which would have been well beyond their reach
- The school administrators were naïve about the government's requirements for creating a school
- The school was built with very limited resources

This story needs to be shared with others not only because it is inspiring, but also because it presents a description of how these people built a school from scratch - equipped it with electricity and running water, jumped through bureaucratic hoops, and created hope for the future of girls who had lost everything.

- Jean Pierce

Why Are You Doing This?

Two factors affected Teresa and Andrew's decision to move from Kenya to the US: the treatment of professors and difficulties experienced in educating their children. Academicians are generally respected in Kenya, but not by politicians. As a result, university lecturers are poorly paid. Nevertheless, Teresa and Andrew tried to make a go of it at first. Meanwhile, their sons attended a low-cost public school – until one of the teachers injured their younger son, Henry. While the family had been in England, the boys had acquired British mannerisms in the way they spoke. Apparently Henry's teacher disapproved of this so much that one day the teacher pinched his ear until it bled.

So Andrew and Teresa began to search for a private school, and they found a Catholic one. Unfortunately, it could only accept their older son, Francis, since there was an opening at his grade level. But there was no room for Henry, who was seven years old. Now Henry was determined NOT to return to the public school, so he decided to stay home while Francis went to school. After about a week, he put on his best clothes and asked to be taken to the Catholic school. He knocked on the priest's door (who was also the principal), saying "Can't you have sympathy for a boy like me who wants to go to school?" In fact, he refused to leave the priest's office until he was admitted to the school.

That solved one problem, but paying for private schooling put a serious strain on the family's finances. At the beginning of the school year, they would take out a loan then work to pay it off during the rest of the year. This meant taking several part-time positions at universities which were widely separated. Andrew needed to ride a bus to two universities, stay there overnight, then return to Nairobi for his regular teaching job.

And still they were not able to save any money to purchase a house. Eventually, the situation became intolerable, and they told themselves they had nothing to lose by starting over in a new country, "If we don't die here, we'll die there." Years later, they recognize the parallel in the desperation they felt and the hopelessness they see in many of the girls admitted to JAMS.

They had friends in Maryland, so they sold everything and emigrated. When they first arrived in Maryland, they found a church where they felt at home. Coincidentally, the pastor had worked for a while in Kenya. Knowing the level of poverty there and the difficulties of creating a home in a foreign country, the pastor asked them what household items they needed. Andrew admitted that they didn't even have plates, "And of course," he kidded, "we could use a car!" He was shocked when the pastor replied that a Ford Tempo had been donated to the church, and it was just taking up space in the parking lot. The first task was to take the car for emissions testing – it failed the inspection. So the pastor and her husband paid $500 for the needed repairs, and drove it over to Teresa and Andrew's apartment. They felt overwhelmed, and they asked what they could do in return. The reply was simply, "Someday you will help someone too."

Andrew credited that experience with making a huge difference in their ideas about giving back to others. He said, "Personally, I did not know that the level of philanthropy was so high in America."

He reflected ruefully on some of their experiences when they had sought funding to start a secondary school for indigent girls in rural Kenya. Wealthy friends in Kenya refused to contribute money to the school, even though they knew that their funds would be matched by Americans. Instead, the Kenyans scoffed, "Why are you doing this?

There is no way you can make money from the school!"

A number of years later, when they were professors in Illinois, they still had the car. A graduate student approached them asking, "Can I buy that car from you?" They answered, "No! We never bought it, and you can't buy it. Just use it." And two years later, the car was returned.

How It All Started

In 2003, four friends from Kenya's Nyanza province who were living in the Chicagoland area thought it would be fun to get together. Each of them knew of one or two others from the Nyanza Province who were living nearby, and soon their number grew to 18 people. Realizing that they had a sizable group which might be able to accomplish something, they brainstormed what needed to be done. Their first project stemmed from a cultural tradition. When a Kenyan dies, it is important for that person to be buried in their homeland. Of course, this can be expensive, so the group pooled their funds and came up with $10,000 to cover the costs. Since they all came from near Lake Victoria, they incorporated under the name, "Sango," which is the original ethnic name of Lake Victoria.

But time passed, and fortunately no one had died, so they began thinking of other ways they could use the money. Teresa urged the group to think about how they might support education. She knew that many children from their region had proven themselves to be bright in primary school, but their families had not been able to afford the costs of secondary school. There were two major problems that afflicted the region. First, it had one of the highest rates of HIV in the country, so there were many orphaned children. Second, the province had been marginalized by the political mainstream in Kenya since many opposition leaders had come from Nyanza. So the federal government tended to ignore their problems; many of their schools were run down; and there was little money for education.

As the other members of the group reflected on their own

experiences, they realized that each of them had depended on someone who had done something which had really helped to further their education. This was a natural cause for Sango to tackle.

Realizing that such groups can get into trouble when members fight to satisfy their own needs, they wisely agreed that none of the students they helped could be related to any of them. Each person in the group was tasked with trying to identify a good candidate from the villages where they had been raised. One person knew a boy who had qualified to be admitted to a national school, but he had no money for fees. He became the first student who benefited from Sango's generosity. In this way, Sango initially funded education for three or four children. But they found that the cause was popular, and other people were willing to contribute, and soon the group was paying for over 40 young people to attend secondary school.

About this time, Teresa began to realize that the boys sponsored by Sango seemed to be doing very well. In fact, 90% went on to attend a university. But over the years, only one of the girls had achieved at the same level. This puzzled the educational administration professor, who vowed to visit schools attended by Sango students. When she interviewed headmistresses, she was told that the girls had no motivation to study. Since someone else was paying for their education, they were not willing to work hard. Of course, this was no fault of the schools, which were doing their best. Nothing could be done.

So Teresa asked the girls why they were not performing well. She quickly discovered that there were at least two basic needs which were not being met for female students – they had no sanitary napkins, and they did not have easy access to transportation. Apparently poverty is harder on girls in the society. Boys are the first to get their needs met, and girls receive whatever is left. In fact, the Sango girls were frequently two to three weeks late in arriving at school, and by then they had missed crucial lessons – particularly in cumulative subjects.

Then there were problems imposed by the schools – such as the institution which demanded that parents of each student pay 5000 shillings so that the school could purchase a bus. Teresa argued that Sango was acting as one set of parents paying for four of the students, so the group should only be charged a total of 5000 shillings. The headmistress retorted that the four teens were not Sango's children, and their parents should be forced to pay the bus fee. If Sango were to pay for their education, then they must pay all of the fees.

So Teresa paid a visit to the District Education Officer. She recounted the rude reception at the school when she had protested that Sango was just trying to help, and they were conscientiously paying the bills on time. The District Officer was well aware of the headmistress, and told Teresa that each day so many people expressed concerns about her that they could talk about the complaints for the next two hours. The hope was that the headmistress would retire soon, but in the meantime nothing could be done.

And so Teresa became frustrated. Sango was contributing a large amount of money for education, but she was not happy with the education which the girls were receiving, and she had little recourse – they could not tell the schools what to do. These concerns began to eat away at her. At the same time, she was pondering where she could have the most impact as an educational administrator. Certainly, there were things that she could accomplish in America; but with the same amount of time, money, and effort, her contributions would be magnified in Kenya.

Her mother, Jane Adeny, had died in 2000. And now, as she considered making a life-altering change, Teresa reflected on lessons she had learned at home. She could hear her mother saying, "If you don't try, you will never know. It is better to start and fail than never to start at all." Both of her parents had worked extremely hard. Her father had been an auditor in Kisumu and her mother had successfully grown sugar cane. No doubt about it, her mother's work ethic had deeply affected Teresa, who was expected to weed and do other tasks in the fields. Jane would say, "If you work to make your body beautiful, you will have no food to eat. You will just be beautiful when you die. How does food get to the table if you sit around?"

Even when the countryside was struggling with a famine, their neighbors knew that the Adeny farm would have crops. What was the secret of her mother's success? She wasted no time or space. She planted continuously, taking advantage of the smallest amount of rain. So when everyone else was in the throes of hunger, they would come to Jane Adeny's farm for food. To this day, some of the hundreds of banana trees which Teresa's mother had planted continue to flourish.

Clearly, land was highly valued in the family. In 1994, after Andrew completed work on his PhD in the United Kingdom, Teresa and he visited her mother in Kenya. At the time, they had two cars. Her mother asked them why they would own two cars when they did not have any land? Land would always be there. And so her mother began to look for a suitable plot for the young couple. Shortly, she contacted Teresa to say that she had found a nice place. It was 10 acres on top of a forested hill, and she had paid a small deposit to put a hold on the land for them. Jane knew that the Kenyan government had given small stipends to college students, and she convinced Teresa that she should invest that money in land, assuring her that she could always sell it. This was not difficult. In fact, 10 acres of land cost less than they earned when they sold one of their cars. It turned out that her mother had counseled them wisely. Teresa estimates that if they were to sell the land today – even if it had not been developed, it would bring 100 times its purchase price.

And so, Teresa knew where she might build something to make a difference in Kenya. The next step was to amass some money for whatever project she would pursue. Every pay period, beginning in 2006, she began saving $1000, and after 10 months of shopping for nothing more than food, she had $20,000. In 2008, her vision began to take shape, and she conducted a "feasibility study" by visiting schools and talking to the students. This experience bolstered her confidence that she could indeed use her money and land to begin her own school. Knowing that this could not be done overnight, she resolved to give herself 10 years and then take stock of how it was going.

Finally, in 2008, Teresa began to share her dream with her friends at Sango. She told them how discouraged she had been that they were spending so much money to educate students; yet they were seeing no results for the girls. Nevertheless, her friends looked at her as if she had two heads. She tried to convince them that she was not talking about a large high school like they saw in America. She wanted to begin a simple Kenyan school. Still they were skeptical.

Not to be dissuaded, in the summer of 2009, Teresa took the money she had saved, and with a lukewarm "blessing" from Andrew, who was less than excited about the project, she headed to the wooded land that she owned in Muhoroni, Kenya. Fortunately, her 25-year-old brother James was eager to help. Together, they decided that they would need to repair their father's tractor to use in clearing the land. And James began to walk around the acreage. To his surprise, he discovered that "squatters" had decided to use some of the land to grow their own crops. In fact, these people had been farming there for at least ten years! While James walked, he kept checking his cell phone, looking for where he could get reception. The top of the hill appeared to be the best location, and he advised Teresa that they should begin building there. Then they would work their way down.

James was a terrific help, since he was extremely handy; and he had taken a course in mechanics. One day they had bought a supply of iron sheets, nails, and wooden boards, which he loaded onto a trailer pulled behind the tractor. At five am the next morning, James and four of his friends began constructing a shed. By 7 pm, the young men had completed a 15' x 20' storage shed. Excited about the progress they had made, Teresa expressed her appreciation by cooking a chicken dinner for the hard workers.

Meanwhile, they had identified a contractor who could oversee the construction. During the first week, they hauled cement from Kisumu and stones from a quarry a half mile away, as well as sand and ballast. By the second week, construction had begun on the first building, which would house four classrooms. James and Teresa helped by keeping the site supplied with water. James also stayed overnight on the grounds to make sure that none of their supplies would "disappear." Teresa made sure that he would keep track of the hours he worked so that she could pay him for his efforts. Within two months, they had built all of the walls. All that remained was to construct the roof and windows, and to do some plastering. It was impressive how much had been created from so little!

But not everyone was thrilled with their efforts. It turned out that a young boy – one of the squatters - had tried to plant some maize where they had decided to build the classroom building. Not being clear about the finer points of who owned the land, he had been distraught when he found that his plans for a corn crop had been destroyed. He took his case to the local chief, who recognized that Teresa clearly had the title to the land. Nevertheless, the chief cautioned that the young boy was likely to make trouble for her unless she paid him off, and so Teresa gave 1000 shillings – the equivalent of $12.50– to the assistant chief to pay the boy.

And yet, one night shortly after that, the boy's mother came to the school building and began throwing stones at it. The next day, Teresa went to visit the mother and asked what the problem was. The mother admitted that she had been drunk, but she had also been angry, because her son had never received the money. It turned out that the assistant chief had pocketed the shillings. This time, Teresa made sure that the chief himself was involved. She gave him another 1000 shillings and watched him pay the boy.

Now it was time to return to DeKalb, Illinois. By this point, she had become very thin. Since they had owned no vehicle other than the tractor, she had been walking six miles each day up and down the hill. It had been hard work, but it clearly was worth it. Teresa was excited about the progress they had made, and took many pictures to show people back in the States.

Her friends and family were suitably impressed. Andrew no longer had any doubts about how serious she was, and he agreed to help keep her dream alive. He took out all of his 401K savings to continue the work.

But there was a serious setback. Soon after Teresa returned to America, she received a telephone call shortly past midnight on a Monday evening. Her sister in Kenya said simply, "God has taken James." Teresa screamed and tried to deny the reality of this nightmare. James couldn't have suddenly died. He was a newly married father of a one-year-old baby. Just that weekend, their niece and aunt had been visiting him at the school, and they were delighted to see how happy he was in dedicating so much of his time and energy to building the school. Then, on Monday morning, he had helped load 50 bags, each weighing 50 kg, onto the trailer behind the tractor. No more than 10 minutes later – just after he had started the old tractor, it lost traction and plunged down a bank into a river, pinning him beneath it.

Teresa was devastated. When she thought about the school she wondered, "What do I do now?" That was just one of many times when she considered stopping the whole endeavor. Was it worth it? Then one night she dreamt that she was with her brother, and he reminded her, "We said we were going to do this, to help so many. It must be done." When she woke up, she had again found her resolve to complete the project.

Andrew and Teresa decided to remortgage the house, and Teresa continued setting aside $2000 each month. One of Teresa's colleagues, Christine Kiracofe, had made a generous donation from her family, so during the summer of 2010, work began on two more buildings - one for a laboratory, a project room, and a library, and the other for two dormitories.

This time, Andrew accompanied Teresa. As a professor of engineering, he had much to offer. Inspired by her brother's sacrifice, Teresa came with a renewed excitement for the project. She worked constantly, using "every bit of energy" each day until the sun went down. By the end of the summer, shrubs had been cleared, three buildings had been completed, and countless trees and flowers had been planted.

In December of 2010, when they returned between semesters, they built a guest house with four bedrooms and two baths. This was where the teachers lived during the first years of the school.

The classroom building is dedicated to James Omondi Adeny, who had picked the location and made so many decisions. Every suggestion he had made had been "spot on" – beginning with starting from the top of the hill and working their way down. He is missed greatly, but his ideas live on.

A Time for Rain, A Time for Drought

Special challenges are caused by weather– especially during this period of climate change. In December, 2012, when the ground was dry and cracked, the rains came with a vengeance. The school is built on the side of a hill, so water can gain momentum and wash away the topsoil. There are several steps that have been taken to guard against flooding and other problems caused by heavy rains. For one thing, trenches had been dug around the buildings. In addition, there is a retaining wall to protect the school from water tumbling down the hill.

Nevertheless, one day, Teresa and Andrew were sitting in the dining room when they heard a sound like a huge roll of thunder. Their first thoughts were that lightning had struck a building. But before they could check it out, water began to rush into the dining room. The retaining wall had collapsed, and all of the water forced its way into and through the room where they sat. It was scary, but fortunately the girls had gone home for Christmas break. So when the rains subsided, the school's founders began the messy tasks of cleaning muddy water out of the eating area and investigating what had happened to the retaining wall. Apparently the builder had not sufficiently reinforced the concrete wall. So when it was rebuilt, they made sure that problem was corrected. And yet within the year, even the stronger retaining wall gave way under the force of another deluge.

This time, they excavated the grounds and installed underground water tanks. Workers dug huge holes, lined them with concrete walls, and coated the walls with waterproof concrete. Many – but not all - of the roofs have gutters which guide the water into the tanks. Even so, the rain can come with such force that occasionally the gutters overflow.

Only once did water get into a classroom. But that problem was solved when they built the walls higher. When the water swept away the top soil, fortunately, it collected in a space which was still part of the JAMS school property, so they could cart it back up the hill to their fields.

"Just Start the School First"

What was the worst headache? The school registration process. Teresa knew without question that what she was about to do was obviously a good thing, so of course everyone would want to help support her goal of starting the school. Right?

Now that the first four buildings had been completed, she went to the District Education Office to find out what needed to be done next. There, she met two women – the District Education Officer and the District Education Quality Supervisor. They seemed to be as excited about the idea as she was, and the very next day they came to visit the site. To Teresa's amazement, they declared "You have built too much! All you need is one room. What you have will be a waste of space if you do not open the school immediately."

Despite their misgivings, the women continued to encourage her. They told her that her next step was to find at least seven students and some teachers. They could not begin the registration process until the school was actually running. This struck Teresa as odd, but the District personnel assured her – "just start the school and figure out the registration process as you go along." This was the middle of February, 2011. Unfortunately, she only had until the beginning of March – two weeks – to find the children and adults if she wanted to get the school registered for the coming year. Otherwise, she would need to wait a whole year.

Recruiting teachers turned out to be relatively easy due to the oversupply of people with teaching degrees in Kenya. Since she was so pressed for time, Teresa was simply looking for anyone who could teach.

Within a few days after she advertised the positions, almost 10 candidates had called her. Many of them came from far away, and they would need housing. Working with the director of a nearby school, Teresa interviewed the applicants and quickly identified her first three teachers.

One was a woman who had a bachelor's degree and had prior experience in a couple of schools. The others were two males. In addition to the teachers, Teresa had recruited two young men who had recently completed high school, one through a Sango scholarship, to serve as caretakers. She had known them previously, and she knew she could depend on them.

Likewise, finding bright girls who were impoverished also took very little time. A friend of Teresa's who lived 100 miles away referred the first four girls. One of the teachers found three more. Since the girls would be staying at the boarding school, the caretakers and Teresa quickly assembled bunk beds in one of the dorms. Teresa decided that she would serve as the first cook. In addition, of course, she was the first headmistress ("matron").

After this two-week whirlwind, Teresa finally had an opportunity to rest and reflect on what she was doing. And the enormity of the task began to overwhelm her. What had she gotten into? Before there had just been walls. Now she was responsible for actual lives. Who would plan meals for all of these people every day? Teresa called her sister-in-law and invited her to help cook and plan meals. But this was just the beginning of problems which must be solved. What would she do when a student got sick? How would she pay for food, for lab equipment, for books? And where would she find money to pay the teachers each month? It was too late to turn back. She had to move forward. She tried to reassure herself with the conviction that she was helping the girls. Whatever happened, she was going to make a positive difference in their lives.

Having already emptied their bank account and taken a second mortgage on their house in DeKalb, Teresa and Andrew turned to dear friends in the states. Diana Swanson, a professor at NIU, was their first "angel." She approached her church and TEACH Girls Global and asked them to contribute funds for the fledgling school. Another early benefactor was Sango. Immediately, they donated enough money to fund a scholarship for a whole year.

Of course, tackling the task of finding personnel for a school before registering the institution meant that anyone who hoped to start a school would have to focus on solving an enormous number of problems before they could turn their attention to anything as mundane as registration. And so the first term went, with the teachers bickering among themselves and physically punishing the girls until Teresa replaced all of the educators.

At the same time, Teresa recognized that she absolutely had to register JAMS school, so she returned to the District office to learn about the next step. She was struck by the fact that the District office could not produce a list of the steps for the procedures. Instead, it appeared that they arbitrarily created new hurdles to leap each time she visited them. This time, Teresa was told that she needed to accomplish registration before June. She invited the District's Public Health Officer to visit the school to verify that she had enough toilets, that the ventilation was sufficient, and that the school met safety standards.

In addition, she would need to complete a form and submit it to the Ministry of Education in Nairobi. Fortunately, she knew just the person who could come to their rescue. Andrew's sister was a lawyer in Nairobi. She agreed to handle the procedure for them and learned that it would cost 10,000 shillings, which is the equivalent of $130. The lawyer sent an office worker to the Ministry of Education to pay the sum and to collect the receipt.

Still, they had no verification of the registration. So the lawyer asked the Ministry of Education for help in completing the process. She was shocked to learn that the ministry had no record regarding the registration. At this point, Teresa came to Nairobi and produced the receipt, only to have the ministry official pronounce that it was a fake! Apparently the lawyer's staff member had encountered one of the less-than-honest government workers in the ministry, and that individual had pocketed the cash. So now Teresa needed to pay another 10,000 shillings. This time, she herself took the funds to the Ministry of Education and collected the correct receipt.

So what was the next step in the process? In order to get the school registered, she must have teachers who were registered. While the teachers at JAMS did indeed have certification, they realized that they would be paid whether or not they were registered with the government, so they had not felt motivated to take that step. What was needed was a copy of their university certificate, an ID, a background check, and a health report.

Unfortunately, Teresa discovered that none of the hospitals in the area had the form required by the Ministry of Health for the health report. And so she turned to a friend's brother who was a doctor. The doctor told her that the process of getting the health reports should be free. Nevertheless it was standard procedure to be charged 3,000 to 4,000 shillings. However, he agreed to handle the task for free if Teresa would drive the 60 miles to his office. Once there, Teresa said that she would happily pay him to complete the forms correctly. As soon as this step was finished, Teresa delivered all of the required forms to the Ministry of Education in Nairobi. She was told that now it would take only one to two weeks to complete the process of registering the teachers.

During the next two months, she found herself regularly commuting the 300 miles from the school to Nairobi – riding on a bus that bumped over crumbling roads - only to find out that there still seemed to be no progress on the registration.

Finally, she tracked down a former friend from college who was working at the Ministry of Education. Now, for the first time, she was told "All you need is a provisional registration, since the school is just beginning." In other words, as soon as she had paid the 10,000 shillings, she should have been given this provisional registration as well as a list of tasks that needed to be accomplished. When Teresa read through the list from the Ministry, she realized that she could prove she had met each of the requirements – including the one that the Ministry assumed would be most difficult – obtaining title to the land.

She was told where she could pick up the provisional license. She called that office and was greeted with, "Your provisional license has been sitting here for months. Where have you been?" When Teresa finally received the provisional registration, the Ministry really was not prepared for her to produce all of the other forms required – including the title. Much to her chagrin, she was informed that she would need to begin the whole process of registration again. And so the year 2012 came to a close.

In 2013, a slightly older but much wiser Teresa initiated the procedure again. This time, when she called in the Health Inspector and Quality Supervisor, she was told that they needed 13,000 shillings for their services. Teresa insisted that this process should be free, and told them to submit a written itemization of the costs. By the time they had prepared this, the cost had been reduced to 7000 shillings. Once again she made the familiar trek to the Ministry in Nairobi. She walked the halls of the Ministry, inspecting each office door until she found the name of a man she recognized.

This friend was in a position of authority, and as soon as he learned that district employees had tried to extort money from Teresa, he was furious. He assured her that she should pay nothing. The district employees were paid sufficiently, and they had all of the resources they needed to accomplish their jobs. So Teresa returned to the district and told the employees that the official at the Ministry had asked for their names so that he could discuss the situation with them. Recognizing that they could be fired, the district employees came to JAMS the following day in a government vehicle and conducted the inspection for free.

Teresa served them a meal, and they assured her that she would get their report in a couple of days. But their office had no electricity right then, so their computers were not working. Teresa replied that she and Andrew would pack up their own fully-charged computers and come to the district office so that the forms could be completed. By the time they arrived at the office with the computers, miraculously the proper form had been completed, but the woman who needed to sign the form was nowhere to be found. Teresa and Andrew waited for the rest of the day, but still no one appeared. At 8 am the next morning, she arrived at her office and signed the form.

In the meantime, Teresa had learned from the Assistant Minister of Education that as soon as she had the correct registration form and evidence that she had completed other requirements, she should receive the registration in 24 hours. So once again she made the now-familiar trek to the ministry of education in Nairobi. This time, she went directly to the person in charge – refusing to go through the registry at the ministry. She announced that she was giving him the forms directly, and she would sit in his office until it was done. Teresa was informed that she would need to return the following week, but she refused, protesting that she only had sufficient funds to spend 24 hours in Nairobi.

The officer told her that he would do his best. Teresa asked that they call her when the form was done, and until then she would wander through the streets of Nairobi. The officer told her that she could call at

2 pm to check on their progress, but she really should not be wandering the streets of Nairobi- it was not safe.

Teresa contacted a friend and they met for lunch. She decided to give the office an extra hour to complete the form, so she returned at three. She was told "Where have you been? The form was ready at noon – we've been waiting for you. You must not be serious about registering your school!"

As graciously as she could, Teresa assured him that she was indeed very serious about making sure that the school succeeded. So the officer told her that the next step was to pick up the completed registration after paying 5000 Kenyan shillings. She was sent to an office which was locked, but finally the staff member showed up at 4:30 pm. Unfortunately, the office would close in half an hour, so there might not be enough time to create the form.

By now, Teresa had encountered a gentleman who appeared to be at the same stage of the process for obtaining registration, but he seemed to be well-connected, and the procedure was going more smoothly for him. She asked him to wait for her. Shortly later, he received his registration, but Teresa was told that she would need to return the following day. The gentleman stepped in and took her defense, saying "This lady has been waiting all day." Finally, Teresa was informed "You are very lucky. Your registration is complete." And she was handed the form certifying that JAMS was registered to serve up to 160 students.

All that she could do was leave the office and drop to her knees in the corridor. The gentleman came to her side, asking "Are you OK?" Teresa told him. "It has taken two years, but my kids finally have a school." In retrospect, she confided that if she had not had students depending on her, she would have given up the process long before.

By now, it was June, 2013. Teresa knew that if the first students were to sit for exams in the fall of 2014, she needed to register for the exam more than a year in advance. While Teresa had been working on obtaining the school's registration, Andrew was completing a form needed for registration with the Kenya National Examination Council (KNEC). On a Thursday, Andrew asked the District Education Officer to sign it and give him some figures so that they could obtain the exam registration. But he was told that they needed to see the school registration which Teresa was bringing from Nairobi. So on Friday, Teresa and Andrew took the school registration to the District Office, only to learn that the District Education Officer would not be in until Monday. She was at home, writing her dissertation. Recognizing a way to meet both of their needs, Teresa called her at home and offered to travel there to help with her dissertation. In turn, the woman would get the forms that Teresa needed. The District Education Officer said, "No problem," and Teresa worked with her on the dissertation all day Sunday.

By Monday at 6 am, Teresa and Andrew were on the road, driving to Nairobi. They arrived at 2 pm. By now, Teresa had developed a visceral reaction to just the sight of government offices like Mitiani House, where the KNEC was located. Immediately, she was directed to the appropriate office, where a man checked her papers, signed the forms and sent her next door, where she was greeted by an official who immediately stamped her form, and informed her "You have everything. We will process the documents and send your password to the District Education Office." Teresa was dumbfounded. The whole procedure had taken less than 30 minutes!

She found Andrew and told him how easy it had been. "I fought so hard for two years for registration, why was this so easy?" Andrew was suspicious and agreed that it did not sound right. Teresa returned to the office, but she was reassured that she had finally found an office with competent employees. By now, it was 3 pm, and there would not be sufficient daylight for a drive of 300 miles back to JAMS, so they stayed overnight and returned to Muhoroni the next day.

Subsequently, a colleague who was impressed with JAMS approached Teresa, asking for her help in creating a comparable secondary school for boys. She told him that she would be happy to assist with every task EXCEPT registering.

Watch Out – She's Crazy!

One thing that works in the favor of someone who would like to start a school in Kenya is that there is no shortage of teachers. The government pays teachers a fixed salary – no matter whether they actually show up to teach. So, even when the school could not provide separate sleeping quarters for the teachers, they had more than enough people apply for the positions. But within the first two terms Teresa began to have second thoughts about the staff that had been hired. She suspected that the teachers were resorting to a discipline technique used throughout the country – caning the students. Corporal punishment is used in practically every school in Kenya – with the exception of the school attended by the President's children.

But Teresa had a different vision. For the first two years when she herself had attended a secondary school named Asumbi Girls, a Canadian woman had served as the headmistress. This educator had taken seriously Maslow's admonition that students can learn only if their basic needs have been met, and she had made sure that the students were well fed. She even obtained films like *The Sound of Music* to entertain the students on weekends. Teresa realized that she and her fellow classmates were happy, and it was easy for them to focus on their education. All this changed in her third form, when the school was run by a woman who did not believe in any of those techniques. Teresa described her last two years in high school as "hell." She discovered how hard it was to try to study when they were only given strong tea. If they wanted bread or sugar, their families would need to provide it. This experience had convinced her to follow the model of the Canadian headmistress if ever she were to open her own school.

In fact, when she greeted the first students at JAMS, she had made their beds; and she gave them a carefully-tied packet containing school uniforms and essential personal care supplies, including sanitary napkins. It is exceptional to find a school in Kenya which ensures that girls are provided with feminine hygiene products so they do not need to miss any time in class.

Then she made sure that they felt empowered to take control of their learning experience. Frequently, she repeated phrases such as, "You are here because you want to learn – not your mother or your father, but you." "This is your school. It is not my school. My school was Asumbi Girls. You must be here because you want to be here." Next she told them how to show that they wanted to be at JAMS: by displaying discipline, by refraining from gossip, and by showing respect for others. Above all, the girls learned to take seriously the words of the *Serenity Prayer*, "grant me the serenity to accept the things I cannot change; the courage to change the things I can; and the wisdom to know the difference." Then she instructed the girls, "Just as I have done this for you, you can repay me by doing this for the next group." So the following year, these first 12 girls followed the same procedure when they greeted the incoming class of students, and now it is expected that all 2nd form students will instill these values in girls entering the 1st form.

So she became concerned when she heard teachers complain that the students were being "spoiled" by the room and board they received at JAMS. Over time, she realized that these teachers disagreed sharply with her vision.

Unfortunately, the teachers she had hired were not prepared to make any sacrifices. They assumed that anyone beginning a school must be wealthy. And besides, Teresa had had enough money to provide bread and mattresses for the students. Now teachers in Kenya expect to be treated with more respect than their pupils. They assumed that obviously Teresa had plenty of money. She simply must be refusing to share it with the adults. The jealousy of the teachers began to boil to the surface. To assert their control over the girls, the adults began to punish by assigning hard labor to any teen who displeased them.

The fact that the fledgling school had no water or electricity did nothing to convince the teachers of the dire straits. At this time, water was fetched from the river. And though there was a generator, gasoline was too costly, so they could not afford to run it. Instead, they used lanterns which required paraffin and hoped that they had sufficient paraffin to last. If they ran out, they were reminded just how pitch black it was at night in rural Kenya.

One classroom did have solar lighting, so the students would stay there until 10 pm. Then they would use lanterns and flashlights to find their ways to their dormitory. Eventually, a friend of Teresa's learned of the situation and gifted the school with 12 solar lamps. Since the school now had 12 students, there was one for each.

Of course, the teachers complained, assuming that they should be the first to get these advantages. So Teresa asked them, "If you had too little food, would you eat before feeding your child?" The teachers replied, "These are not our children." But Teresa assured them that the girls were like her own daughters.

Once, when Teresa was away from the school, the kitchen ran out of bread. As soon as they learned of the problem, the teachers bought enough bread so that they could eat, but not enough for the girls. When Teresa returned, she bought just enough bread for the girls. Again, the teachers complained that the girls would not respect them. They challenged her, saying "Why do we have to pay for our own bread when you give it to the students?" Teresa replied, "This school is for the students."

Another time, Teresa found that she could get a good deal if she purchased more than one or two pairs of slippers at a time. They really were "cheaper by the dozen." So she bought enough for all of the girls. The students were so proud of their slippers that they put them on early one evening. As soon as the teachers saw this, they scolded the girls, saying "You are so pampered. It is too easy for you. You won't pass your exams." After that, the girls only wore the slippers on weekends, when the teachers were not at the school.

Eventually, it became evident that the teachers wanted to be treated as the ultimate authorities. Not only would they be the source of all knowledge, but they expected students to be dependent on them to dispense supplies for hygiene, etc. In fact, they prevented the students from having access to the books which were donated by BookFriends and by the Barrington Rotary Club. When Teresa discovered that, she told the girls that they should go to the library to read about whatever topic they were studying, and then go to class, prepared to ask questions. The students took her advice, but then Teresa discovered that the teachers felt threatened by students who would challenge them by saying, "but I read this...."

The school had opened in March of 2011. The 2nd term was drawing to a close in June. Teresa realized that soon her sabbatical would be coming to an end, and she would need to return to Northern Illinois University in August. She began to feel very uneasy about what kind of school she was leaving behind. She realized that some of the teachers were simply trying to "wait her out," and as soon as she left, they would resume caning the girls. These concerns multiplied until one day she made a seemingly split second decision. She called all of the teachers together and informed them that they ALL were being fired.

Everyone – including Andrew – was shocked at what she had just done. She even heard that people in the local community were calling her "crazy" for this impetuous act. So Teresa invited the local leaders to meet with her, and she explained why she had taken such a radical step, "If you want your children taught by someone who acts like that, then you can take them elsewhere –to any other school. But if I do not correct the situation right now, it will always be this way." Eventually, the neighbors came to agree with her.

July was spent interviewing new teachers. She made sure to tell each the philosophy of the school – that the teachers and students are expected to learn together – that they must be able to work together. Fortunately, she discovered that her headmaster understood and agreed with her, and together they were able to staff the school with like-minded educators. In addition, Teresa knew that she could trust two aids who stayed at JAMS and were able to give her regular reports on the school climate.

So now when a bright student like Abigail challenges teachers by asking a question, they realize that they need to turn it around, asking, "What do you think?" and they need to be willing to recognize that frequently her perspective is correct. If she happens to be wrong, they invite her to research the correct answer and share it with the class.

In December, 2012, when Teresa was chatting with individual staff members, one male teacher told her, "I don't like teaching this class. They act like they know everything." Teresa replied, "You should be flattered. This is not a negative thing. You have helped them learn." Another male teacher said that he felt badly that three of the girls in his class were smarter than he was. Teresa assured him, "It is OK. You are the facilitator. Your job is to help them find the answers.

In other schools in Kenya, girls tend to be timid. They have many needs which are not being met. Furthermore, much of the teachers' time is devoted either to disciplining students or to helping them find food and basic supplies. But at JAMS, since the girls' needs have been met by the school, when they go to class they have time to learn – all they need is an education.

And all of the teachers at JAMS know that at any time – that "crazy" person who started the school could fire any and all of them.

"Mommy"

The teaching staff showed respect for Teresa by calling her "Director." But the initial students did not know what to make of her. The first four girls recalled the time they met Teresa – when she arrived in a 4-wheeled pickup truck to take them to the school. They had imagined how she would look. She would be fat and well-dressed, since she must have a lot of money to begin a school.

They were not prepared to see a slender woman, wearing an ordinary house dress and "Crocs." Her legs were streaked with mud, since she had come directly from working on the school. The girls were very confused. If she is so dirty, what must the school look like? And why would someone who is dirty be driving a 4-wheel pickup?

The more they got to know her, the more they became convinced that Teresa was a series of contradictions. Here was the Director who owned the school. Yet she had short hair like the girls, and she was dressed in ordinary clothes, so she must not be affluent. Moreover, in the early days, Teresa stayed in the dorm with the girls. Since she was old enough to be their parent, they began to call her "Mom."

One day in 2013, Teresa opened her ipad, which had photos taken at her son Henry's graduation. The girls who stood near her looked shocked.

Teresa tried to reassure them, "Yes, I have a son who is that old."

But one replied, "It's not that. We didn't know you were so beautiful!" Others chimed in, "Is that you?!" "No. It's not her!"

Teresa began to wonder whether they were looking at the same picture. But it was indeed her family, and she pointed to each one, "Here is my son, my husband, and me."

The girls exclaimed, "You left that life to come here?!"

Indeed, one of the most puzzling things that the girls learned about "Mommy" was that she was a professor who lives in the United States. They were amazed that a woman of such means would dress so simply and keep her hair short. And so the whole idea of simplicity in the school began to take root.

When the girls debated whether to have long or short hair in the school, they noted that Teresa had resources, and yet she kept her hair short like the poorest Kenyans, so why should they bother with expensive hair products?

Four of the girls who attended the school in the first years did come from relatively wealthy families. Their fathers had professional careers. For a variety of reasons, these girls had not been realizing their potential in other schools, so they were referred to JAMS.

When Teresa first met the daughter of one of these men, the girl had brought her clothes packed neatly in a suitcase. Teresa asked her, "Why did you bring a suitcase and your own clothes? You are here to learn. We provide uniforms and a weekend dress. You just need to work hard." And she added, "You aren't staying here because your father wants you to. You have to want to be here." And she invited the girl to walk around the compound, observing what was different from her previous school. The girl returned and reported that she liked the library, the dorm, the girls, and the food.

Then Teresa said, "You don't need your long hair and fancy clothes or even expensive sanitary napkins here." Simple clothing and personal supplies were all provided by JAMS. So the girl was given one week to decide whether she wanted to attend the school and whether she was willing to cut her hair. Two days later, the girl returned with short hair. Subsequently, she was given an opportunity to grow in areas beyond academics. She earned the respect of the other students by singing in talent shows. And eventually she learned to respect the other girls for being bright, creative, and nice despite their humble backgrounds.

So the girls embraced the simplicity at JAMS school. More than one student has exclaimed, "We don't have good roads, but a professor lives here!" They learned that simplicity does not indicate that people are necessarily poor. In fact, this school is good enough for both, rich and poor girls. Recently, a girl who was newly-admitted to the school was staying at JAMS for an orientation before the other students would return from Christmas break. She had experienced a very difficult life, and she clearly defined herself as being really poor. But as soon as the other girls started to arrive, the newcomer realized she had a lot in common with them, and she began to shed her self-pitying view of herself as a victim. She asked, "Will I become like you soon?" And the day she received her uniform, she could not stop smiling. She did not want to take it off.

Indeed, the values of the school transcend differences in wealth – honesty, dignity, and integrity. This makes a strong impression on the girls, who show their appreciation for "Mommy" in many small ways. No sooner would she remove her shoes than someone would clean them. They even compete to wash her dresses and make her bed. Teresa would tell them. "I do not want to know who did that. You did it because you wanted to." And so a culture of mutual caring in the midst of simplicity was created at the school. In this environment, the students behave not because they fear being whipped or expect to receive reinforcements. They know that here their basic needs are met, with a particular focus on the need for love and respect.

"Don't You Have School Rules?"

One day during the summer of 2013, representatives of the Ministry of Education visited JAMS to evaluate the school. One of the questions which they routinely ask students during such visits is "Can you tell us the school's rules?" The assumption is that a school where students cannot recite the rules has no discipline.

One after another, girls at JAMS were stymied when the evaluators posed this question, and the government regulators demanded, "Don't you have school rules?" Then a teacher spoke up, saying that the girls had heard the rules, but they do not break them, so there is no need to repeat them over and over. Following the rules had become part of their lives. And the teacher asked the girls, "How many discipline problems have you seen?" and "How many of you have been caned?" When the girls responded that they had neither witnessed discipline problems nor been caned, the school evaluators were shocked.

Clearly, the climate of mutual respect at JAMS school is not typical in the country. In fact, two days a week, the girls wear trousers to class. This is unheard of in most Kenyan schools, since pants are associated with power. People communicate their status as ministers, directors, senators, etc. when they wear slacks. Their daughters attend private schools where they are allowed to wear pants. At first, the girls at JAMS were hesitant, but they quickly learned that they could feel new-found freedoms to bend over and pick up something or to sit comfortably. Now they choose to wear trousers when they compete against students from other schools. They have found that the boys from the other schools really do view them as competitors because of the way they are dressed.

To illustrate the degree to which students are trusted and empowered to make decisions at the school, Teresa notes that the girls are frequently invited to debate the merits and demerits of potential school policies. For instance, soon after the school opened, one of the first issues concerned whether the students would have long or short hair. Rather than telling the girls what they needed to do, Teresa asked the girls to debate the issue and assured them that the majority decision would be honored. So the girls researched the issue and presented relevant arguments. Some noted that long hair requires expensive products, using money needed for other essentials. Others observed that their daily schedule was so full, they really did not have the time needed to care for long hair. (Andrew insists that everyone must sleep for at least 8 hours, so lights out is at 10 pm; they awake at 6 am; and they eat breakfast at 7.) Finally, someone reported that lice can hide in long hair, and this causes problems for everyone. When all of the arguments had been heard, Teresa drew a line down the center of the room. She told them that all in favor of long hair should stand on one side of the line, and those opposed on the other side. All except two students crossed to the "short hair" side of the line. This is as authentic as it gets when "problem-based learning" is an instructional methodology.

Another time, Teresa and Andrew realized that the girls were falling asleep in classes following lunch. The girls were presented with this problem and were asked how to solve it. They studied their current meal time routine – typically followed in boarding schools in Kenya – porridge for breakfast, maize and beans for lunch. They determined that their lethargy was caused by the meal of maize and beans. So the girls concluded that they needed to eat rice for lunch so that they could stay awake during class. Then they would have maize and beans for dinner.

Clearly, critical thinking is valued at the school. The girls are taught that they can report a minor problem to a staff member only <u>after</u> they have tried to solve it. (minor problems do not involve abuse). They are also taught how to take responsibility. So for instance, they are expected to leave the indoor bathroom clean enough that "Mommy would be willing to eat a meal there." Although the facilities are indoors, they can best be described as footprints, designating where one squats. So each girl brings a bucket of water to flush and clean. If a girl enters the facility and notices that it is not clean, she is expected to find the previous occupant and show her how to clean it. Students are warned that if they were to omit this step and immediately tattle to a staff member, both they and the offending student would be sent home.

This is not to say that every student has succeeded at JAMS. Three of the first 60 students either left or were expelled. One had slapped another student, another had refused to cut her hair. A third student was nasty towards the others. When she returned home to her family, she fabricated complaints about the school in an effort to manipulate her aunt to send her to a day school. When her aunt was invited to stay overnight at JAMS, she understood just how troubled her orphaned niece had been.

Reinforcement is not the first choice for teaching students how to act, though it is used occasionally. When Teresa visits the school during June and July, students are recognized with two types of awards. The first is a "queen cake," which is a prized cup cake. This is given to anyone in form 2 who is identified by students in form 1 as being particularly helpful to them.

The second is an award that goes to the student who is voted "outstanding." This is the girl who most embodies the school's motto "Grow in Wisdom," and who lives the *Serenity Prayer*. Not only does this student perform well in class, but she goes way beyond to help others. The girls are reminded that they must be truthful when they cast their votes – not just vote for their best friend. Teresa was convinced that the girls had taken the vote seriously in 2013 when they elected Bonnie. At first, Teresa was puzzled by the vote. Bonnie had been identified as bright by Agape, an organization that focuses on rehabilitating "street children." But she was very quiet, and she had not fit in initially. Since she had not grown up in a rural area, she seemed to be weak and could not even balance water on her head. Instead, she fell repeatedly. Eventually, she developed the strength to master this task. Learning how to overcome this problem seemed to have a strong effect on her, and though she continued being very quiet, Bonnie was recognized as a person who would look for anyone who seemed to be struggling in class. Immediately, she would come to their aid and offer to help them learn how to cope until they succeeded.

Carol

Carol was one of the first four girls admitted to the school. She came from a small farm, where she lived in a hut with both parents and seven brothers and sisters. As the oldest daughter in the family, she had learned how to be a mother to her siblings. And at JAMS, the teachers immediately saw her leadership potential. She was the one who would volunteer, "We need to clean in the morning." Once, she noted, "We need a timetable for eating." Then, before an adult could react, Carol produced a draft of the needed form. So naturally, she was nominated to be the "head prefect" for the students.

Now prefects tend to have a lot of power, and in some schools prefects have been known to accept bribes or even to cane the other children. But Carol was different.

Although – or perhaps because - she came from a large, poor family, she did not ask for anything; and she appreciated whatever she was given. She would think nothing of sharing her clothes with others. Once a new girl came to JAMS at a time when school uniforms were out of stock. Unbeknownst to Teresa, Carol gave one of her two skirts to the new girl.

The fact that Carol had a big heart was not lost on the other students. When Teresa asked the students, "Who treats you well?" The girls replied, "I like Carol. She's not corrupt like our country's leaders. She will do things for you without expecting anything in return."

This caught Teresa off guard as she reflected, "What kind of society are we living in? But what an amazing example this girl has been for the other students." Teresa credits Carol with helping to set the tone for the culture of the school. Successive levels of incoming students became aware that they were expected to behave like her.

Once, Teresa had made sure that the girls had a clock in their dormitory. But there had been nowhere to hang it, so she had left it on a bed. It had remained there for a while, but one day, when no one else was around, Carol picked up the clock to see it better. Accidentally, she dropped it, and it broke. Immediately, she went to Teresa and confessed, saying that she wanted to be the first to tell an authority – even though no one else had seen her. She knew that the school had a policy of "You break it, you buy it."

But Teresa was so impressed at the girl's honesty, that she said the school would pay for a new clock. Then Teresa called all of the girls together and told them what had happened. She said that Carol had immediately confessed to the accident, so she would not need to pay for the clock.

Several months later, Teresa saw that a table in the library was broken. This time, no one admitted to causing the problem. So Teresa told them, "All of us are responsible for buying a new table. We will not purchase bread for a week, and then we will have saved enough to replace the table. After the week, a group approached her and told how the table had been broken. Apparently the girls had been watching a video, when a number of them had tried to sit on the table. Now the tables and chairs that Teresa had bought were not very heavy, so they would not create indentations in the concrete floors. And naturally the table had collapsed. But the girls had been in a darkened room, and no one was sure just who had broken the table.

When the whole student body was assembled, Teresa asked them, "If you sat on that table, please stand up." A lot of the girls stood up, and Teresa told them all that from then on, no one could sit on a table.

Soon after, the school was gathered for an assembly. In the middle of the event, Teresa heard the girls gasp. When she asked what was wrong, the students told her that a teacher was sitting on a table. Immediately the teacher got up, and Teresa told her, "That's good. If you had broken it, you would have paid for a new one."

And so, the students have learned to appreciate that they need to take care of the things the school provides for them. In most boarding schools, thin mattresses last for just one year. But already the mattresses at JAMS are still in good shape after three years, and it is hoped they will last another three or four years. One reason that they are in such good condition is that Carol makes sure the girls do not bounce up and down on their beds. This really has not required strong policing on her part. When bedtime comes, they are usually too tired to do anything but sleep!

Doris

Doris, Carol, Ellen, and Fran were the first four girls who enrolled in the school. This is the story of Doris.

Both of her parents had died by the time she was five, so Doris went to live with her mother's sister. (In Kenya, the father's sister is called "Aunt," but the mother's sister is called "Mom"). But within five years, Doris's second mom developed a brain tumor, and she also died. So at the age of 10, Doris had lost three parents, and she was invited to live with another maternal sister. Understandably, adjusting to each successive loss and transition had been very traumatic for the young girl.

This couple welcomed Doris, thinking she could help around the house. But the husband quickly realized how bright Doris was, so he was willing to pay for her to go to primary school. At the age of 15, as soon as Doris had completed primary school testing, her uncle announced that he had helped the girl enough, and it was time for her to return to the hometown where she had been born. Supposedly, her grandfather lived there, and Doris could stay with him. But actually, the grandfather was known as a "wanderer" who could not stay in one place very long.

Having left this "hometown" 10 years earlier, Doris knew no one else, and so she was left to her own devices to survive. Since she was resourceful, she began to pick as much sugar cane as she could carry. She would pay a basic amount to the farmer, and then she could sell the rest for as much as she could make. People in the community began to realize that she was clever but too poor to afford secondary school, and they took pity on her.

About this time, Teresa had turned to a friend to help recruit girls for the school. Her friend contacted four headmasters of schools in Doris's hometown. They identified the 15-year-old as a strong candidate for JAMS school, and gave the friend a photo of Doris. Life was looking up for the young girl who began to anticipate continuing her education. In the meantime, the friend's brother died, and this consumed all of her time, energy, and attention. So much so that by the time school was starting, Teresa's friend had totally forgotten about Doris. Fortunately, the head masters did not give up. They contacted Teresa, telling her this was Doris's only chance. "If she can't go to school, what else can she do?" So Teresa called Andrew and explained Doris's plight. He, in turn, dialed Diana, who described the situation to people at her church. Immediately, Diana's church agreed to sponsor this girl who had so much potential. For her part, Teresa had purchased a full set of clothes and shoes for Doris, and the girl was ready to begin high school.

Knowing that Doris had managed to attract supporters and she had a chance to succeed, her uncle suddenly showed up one day, saying that now he was willing to be part of Doris's life once again. But Teresa told him, "If you show up, then you need to pay for her education." The uncle disappeared, never to be seen again at JAMS school.

Some children, when repeatedly confronted with the loss of significant family members, begin to blame themselves. Others tend to become outwardly angry with the world. By the time she came to JAMS, Doris's anger boiled just below the surface.

One day, the students were talking about how they should accomplish the task of carrying water from the river to the trees. Carol suggested, "Rather than making a lot of trips, let's take large buckets. We are big girls."

Doris retorted, "If you're a big girl, you should be married by now." This led to some sharp words, and Doris ended the argument when she hit Carol with a bucket.

Now Teresa had been away from the school when this happened, so she knew nothing of the situation. When she returned to JAMS, she had work to do in her office while school was in session. But she looked up from her task to see Doris digging in the fields. Angrily, Teresa confronted the teachers, saying that NO ONE should be outside while class was in session. They told her about the altercation, and they ended by saying that they were using a standard practice in Kenya –punishing a student during class.

Teresa called Doris into her office and said, "You need to be very honest with me. I don't want to hear the story from anyone else."

Doris replied, "I'm so sorry. I don't know what came over me."

Realizing that the girl might have been resorting to behaviors that were an accepted part of her childhood, Teresa asked what had happened when she had made a mistake as a little girl. Doris reported a lifetime of being beaten by people using any object that had been handy. She concluded by protesting, "But I did apologize to Carol."

Teresa counseled her, "You can stay at this school for four years. But this was your last chance to hit anyone. You have spent your one and only chance to act like that."

Citing a passage in the Bible, Doris replied, "I would rather cut off my hand than lift a finger against someone again."

Now all of the students had known about the incident, so Teresa called them together, saying, "This was a learning experience for ALL of us. If anyone ever lifts a finger against someone else at this school again, you will be sent home immediately. Doris is not going home this time, since we are all learning from what happened."

This event had a profound effect on Doris, and the story became part of the school's lore. So when another girl took out her anger by slapping a classmate who was sleeping, the aggressor was immediately discharged from the school.

Gert

The towns nearby JAMS are close-knit, and when Doris was accepted at the school, word quickly traveled around the community. Gert lived at home with her father, who had been a paraplegic since birth. He could not sit for long, but he could repair clothes at a sewing machine, and this allowed him to pay for food for his large family.

Now Gert had not proven herself to be an outstanding student during primary school. Nevertheless, she was determined to go to high school. Her father had managed to get a son admitted to the local secondary school by promising to pay his tuition, but he had not been able to make good on the promise. The headmaster had permitted the boy to remain at the school. But when Gert approached him, he refused to accept another child from the family. So each day, Gert would sit outside an open window of the school, and would try to learn whatever she could hear – until she was discovered and ordered to leave.

This went on for some time, and then Gert learned about Doris's story and about Teresa's friend who had tried to help. Gert knew where the woman lived – six miles away. So one day at 5 am, she put her father in his wheel chair, and she began to wheel him the whole distance – over muddy and rutted roads. They arrived at the friend's house at 8 pm, and by then the father and daughter were both too exhausted to talk coherently.

Finally, Teresa's friend realized that Gert was hoping to be admitted to JAMS. But the friend said that she had no idea whether the school was still accepting students. The desperate father announced that he was going to find a way back to their village, but he was leaving Gert with the friend, and if the school had no room then the girl would just have to work for Teresa's friend.

After the friend heard this story, she decided that she must raise enough money to at least take Gert to JAMS. By now, Teresa was not sure where she could turn for tuition money for Gert, and clearly the girl was impoverished. Apparently Gert's family had been so poor that she did not even have her own underpants. But she did have shoes. Yet every night, Gert would wash out her socks. So when the girl was not looking, Teresa turned over one of her shoes and saw a huge hole in the sole. She learned that the girl wore a size 7 shoe, and the next time Teresa went to town, she went to a second hand shop and found some shoes in the correct size. She told the girl, "I was walking around the market today and picked up these for you." Gert was thrilled with the gift.

Still, no one had agreed to pay her tuition. Her father did promise to send what he could, and after a month, he did give Teresa 800 shillings ($10 US). But that was all that he could afford. Tuition costs $800 per year.

Then Teresa's son, Henry, heard about Gert's story when he was working as a barista at Starbuck's. As a student at Northern Illinois University, he could empathize with Gert, who had a passion to learn. Henry had set a goal of earning a law degree, so he knew what it was like to work hard for a goal. He convinced some friends to help him raise $400 each year, and his parents would match the amount to pay Gert's tuition.

Once the girl earned only a grade of "C" and Teresa told her, "Remember that my son's money is paying for you to attend school."

So Gert wrote directly to Henry, saying, "Please don't drop me! I'm doing my best."

And Henry told his mother, "If she's doing her best, that's OK."

Gert was very quiet, and Teresa was convinced that she could improve her English if she spoke more frequently, but this seemed to be extremely difficult for the girl. When Teresa finished telling this story, she considered what the future holds for "average" students like Gert. Research has shown that high school graduates do tend to have fewer children, and their families are healthier. And JAMS is developing plans to teach the students skills like how to raise animals, bake bread, and sew sheets. In addition, Gert might become a trainee for an NGO which recruits people to educate others about their civic rights and responsibilities or about how to protect themselves from AIDs and other sicknesses.

Farm Animals, Feathers, and Fins

One of Teresa's goals for JAMS has been to make the school as self-sustaining as possible. The girls who come from surrounding farms are already highly skilled at tilling the ground, and the school grows some basic crops. In addition, she has investigated how to raise animals. One of the most challenging of these projects has been creating a dairy.

Trevor Tomkins, a member of the Friends of JAMS Board, has been instrumental in helping the school to plan and develop the dairy. Ground was broken for the initial structure in the summer of 2014, and the dairy was slated to be operational by the end of 2014. Unfortunately, that date had to be postponed. The owner of a large dairy (over 1000 cows) had offered to donate four to JAMS. But at the time, the school's facilities were not completed, so he agreed to wait. He told Trevor's consultant, "When you are ready, just come." By December, JAMS was ready, but by then, the owner was in Europe for the holidays. While he returned, he discovered that his manager had engaged in malpractice, and the firm had lost funds. So the consultant began to look for cows to purchase, using donations of $4000 raised by Kirsten Torgerson, a Cornell University student who designed the dairy. These efforts were delayed when it was discovered that foot and mouth disease had ravaged dairies nearby, so she would not be able to purchase cows from them until June.

The plan was to purchase two pregnant cows and one that was lactating. So the girls would learn how to care for the cows from birth through milking. Teresa grew up on a farm, so she was well-aware of the role of a midwife to a cow. She described how first she would rub her hands in ash, then pull slowly on the calf's head and legs.

The cows would be fed a steady diet of corn, millet, and grass. Part of the learning process involved creating silage. When Teresa returned to the school in December, 2014, a machine designed to process the feed had arrived, and the corn was getting dry. It had to be crushed before it spoiled. Once the corn is cut, it must be processed immediately, mixed with molasses, and stored in huge, airtight plastic bags. So for two days, 12 people worked for up to 10 hours a day and created five tons of silage. That would be enough to feed four cows for three months. (In the future, people will be hired to do this task.)

For the first year, the dairy would be run by a manager from Trevor's Venture Dairy. If, at the end of that time, the girls are ready to control the operation, the manager will leave. Eventually, the goal is to have 20 cows at JAMS, and to supply milk not only to feed the girls but to sell to the neighbors. Unfortunately, the consultant had ordered 300 bales of hay when she thought that the cows were coming momentarily. She had obtained it for a good price, but of course now there was a question about whether it would keep. They had a mountain of hay – way too much to store in a barn. But fortunately, the rains were delayed, so the hay did not spoil.

But the cows produce more than milk, so there are also plans to create biogas from processing the manure (no, the gas does not smell!). Just four cows should help produce enough fuel to cook for the whole school.

In addition to producing their own milk, the school has invested in chickens. This too has brought its own set of challenges. When the school was first started, Andrew had built a chicken coop which worked very well to protect the chickens at night. In the morning, baby chicks would wander outside of the coop and head for some straw. Unfortunately, hawks learned to wait patiently, and when the chicks ventured out, the hawks would swoop in for their own breakfast.

So Teresa consulted experts about the dimensions and construction required for a chicken house. And, with a donation from one of JAMS' generous supporters, the coop was built. But, in Teresa's words, "Somehow, everything we build winds up bigger than expected!" and this was the case with the chicken coop. Meanwhile, Andrew was sent to pick up 100 chickens. Unfortunately, by the time he returned to JAMS, only 65 had survived the 40-mile trip. Apparently the company had jammed too many into a box, and the rest had suffocated.

Raising chickens is important to the school because their eggs had been coming from South Africa. But now they needed a cost effective way to provide chicken feed. Buying feed locally proved to be more expensive than importing the eggs!

Fortunately, the machine purchased to produce feed for the cows can also be used to make chicken feed. The school uses the corn which they grow and adds supplements which they buy. In the future, the school might be able to sell chicken feed in the local markets. In addition, the same machine could be used to grind corn for the porridge served in the dining room.

Teresa did have more luck creating and stocking tilapia fish ponds. Other schools have tried to create artificial ponds with plastic lining, and these have not worked very well. During the rainy season, the ponds would fill with mud, and the fish would die. So Teresa learned how to create more sustainable ponds. She discovered that a pond only needed to be two to three feet deep, and that it should be placed next to a large tree in such a way that the shade from the tree would protect the pond during the heat of the day. Then she and Andrew visited Will Allen, winner of a MacArthur award to create a sustainable farm in Milwaukee. They observed how hydroponics are managed to grow plants while recycling water, so they do not need to continuously cart water from the river. Now the water from the pond with fish waste is pumped through roots of vegetables, which serve as a filter and infuse oxygen into the water before it is circulated back to the pond.

They brought in 600 fish. But oddly, the fish seemed to disappear as soon as they were put in the water. There was no sign of life for the first three days. So Teresa turned to experts, who reassured her that the fish had gone to the bottom of the pond, where they were simply trying to acclimatize to the strange surroundings. By the fourth day they showed up when food was available, and from then on the fish could be seen whenever they expected to be fed. The experts were impressed that fewer than 15 fish were lost during this process.

But keeping the water suitable for the fish to survive would not be easy. The water would need to be drained through an outlet at the bottom of the pond while new water was added every two weeks (there is a retaining pond so no fish are lost while this is going on). In addition, the water needed to be aerated, so Andrew brought a solar pump for this purpose, but their car was broken into, and the first pump was stolen.

And then there were birds with long beaks which sat patiently in a tree above the pond. One worker spent the whole day chasing a particularly determined bird which returned every 15 minutes, ever hopeful of a tasty tilapia meal. Even the tree itself began to pose problems for the pond. Its large leaves fell into the water and begin to disintegrate, releasing toxic chemicals. So the next step was to build a 2-meter wall around the perimeter of the ponds and to cover it with chicken wire. In addition, they needed to dig a third pond. After six months, when the first fish reached maturity, newborn fingerlings would be endangered. (Who knew that tilapia eat their young?).

In addition, the school owns some sheep. Teresa would like for the school to be able to slaughter one lamb each month to supplement the girls' diet. But first she needs to convince the school's managers of the wisdom of this plan, since the practice challenges the cultural norm of accumulating animals simply to demonstrate one's wealth.

Finally, the school owns three goats – although Teresa entered into this transaction very reluctantly. A neighbor needed money, so she sold one of the goats to JAMS. Though Teresa wanted to help the neighbor, she had no intention of letting a goat destroy the grounds of the school. So Teresa offered to pay for veterinary costs and for the cost of a roof over the woman's house, and in return the neighbor agreed to house the goat. This proved to be a very expensive goat! However, the goat did give birth to twins.

Micro Grants and Cottage Industries

Not only do Trevor and Teresa value growing healthy foods for the students, but they have a broader vision. Trevor remarked, "The benefits will be much larger for these young girls' communities as they take their new-found skills home. Small dairy farms that produce good quality milk start to generate an income and take people from subsistence to small-scale commercial businesses."

Another part of the long-range plan is for some girls to receive micro grants while they learn how to care for the animals and engage in other "cottage industries."

One of the school's major benefactors, Larry Barnett, in conjunction with the Rotary club of Barrington, Illinois, provided money for the school's well. Now he is turning his attention to raising $61,000 which will be used to give micro grants to 16 students enrolled in two area schools. Eight of these will be JAMS students. The plan is that the micro loan will pay for their education for the first two years, while they learn how to care for animals or bake or sew, and then the salary they receive for these tasks will pay for their fees during the last two years of high school. No doubt, helping to pay for their education will give the girls a real sense of pride. In addition to learning the skills needed for each of these jobs, the students will work with their teachers to create a schedule for caring for the animals, and they will master business management techniques of record-keeping.

Once again, the best laid plans seem to run into interesting complications in Kenya. Although the Rotary Club in Barrington, Illinois, had met its target by saving the money needed for micro loans, the counterpart club in Kenya has been out of compliance. They cannot access the money for the school until they fix some problems.

When that money becomes available, JAMS will be able to expand its programs.

One of these programs is bread-baking. Teresa had bought an oven for this purpose. Previously, the school had purchased its bread from an outside vendor located 40 miles away, but the students pronounced that their bread was so full of holes that it tasted and felt like "air." Now Teresa created a separate account for baking. The school would pay less for the bread baked in Teresa's oven. But there was still enough to pay for the oven and to purchase ingredients – flour, sugar, oil, and yeast. Not only were the girls learning how to bake, but they were also responsible for the accounting. Soon there would be enough money to purchase another oven.

In the future, it is hoped that students will learn how to sew duvets. Fortunately, Andrew was able to buy a very sophisticated sewing machine at a garage sale in DeKalb, and Teresa found a very light, synthetic material in Malaysia. She is thinking that duvets would be easier to clean than the blankets which they currently use. So in the summer of 2015, the goal is to purchase two additional sewing machines and to attract a tailor who can work with the girls on weekends.

Teresa has a candidate in mind – a woman who is currently sewing uniforms for the school. She has proven that she can accomplish this task cheaper and more efficiently than male tailors. Apparently male tailors in the region think that women are ignorant and try to take advantage of them. So Teresa was delighted to find this woman in the market and to discover that she charges half as much as men and provides beautiful uniforms within a week. Many people in the region depend on buying second-hand clothes, so the woman is delighted that JAMS can keep her busy sewing uniforms.

In fact, she would like to begin teaching home science courses in cooking and housekeeping, in addition to tailoring; but it will take a lot of money to purchase the electric ovens and other equipment.

In addition, Teresa would like to create a greenhouse so that the school can grow its own food despite the droughts and rains that plague the region. She admits, "I'm taking risks. I don't know what will happen in the future, but I must try things like this. Other schools are asking how to do it."

The Costs of a Secondary Education

Kenya has many primary schools which are close enough to villages that children can walk to them. But most of the secondary schools board the students. This happens for a variety of reasons. If the students lived at home, they would be required to spend a lot of time working for the family, and their studies would suffer. In addition, many families which live in cities prefer to send their children to remote areas, where they are less like to leave the school and get distracted by "city lights."

And JAMS is located in about as remote a location as possible. Even Teresa had doubts at first. She knew that the effort might fail, but at least she would have tried. And Andrew confessed, "I thought she was crazy. But now we're in deep, and there is no stopping." People in the village often remark that they had never imagined that the school would succeed.

Even so, they are constantly confronted with new and different problems to solve – most of them relating to costs of providing a secondary education to impoverished children. Just the books for secondary schools are far more expensive than those for primary schools. And certainly more advanced students need costly laboratory equipment and other specialized learning resources. Then of course, when the expenses of providing room and board are added, there is little money left over.

They have learned to be frugal, so usually the people at JAMS are very good at coping. But when Teresa returned to the school in May, 2013, she encountered a problem that went well beyond their resources – the prospect of paying for extracurricular opportunities.

Some of the girls were developing special talents in music and in soccer. In fact, teams from JAMS had experienced success when they competed with students from other schools. They had beaten other schools in soccer, and they had won first prize in choral performances. The students were excited. They were eagerly anticipating and practicing hard for future competitions. But this all came as a surprise to Teresa, and when she arrived at the school, she was greeted with the news that the girls would need approximately 80,000 shillings – the equivalent of $1000 – in order to compete at a musical competition at the regional level. This would cover the costs of transportation, registration, meals, allowances for chaperones, etc.

Teresa was floored – the school had no money in the budget for a $1000 one-day trip. So she met with the girls. They tried every argument they could imagine – including the fact that competing favorably would make more people aware of the school. This was a strong consideration, but Teresa had to make them understand, "We are really struggling to keep things going. As much as I like what you have done, we simply cannot make that trip. But I am open to your suggestions for how we could raise 80,000 shillings."

So the girls began to brainstorm. They even suggested that the school could cut back on the cost of food – they would voluntarily miss meals for a week. But Teresa assured them that none of their ideas would generate enough money. The only way that there would be sufficient money would be if some of the talented girls could convince their families to pay for the trip. This could have been feasible for at least one of the girls, whose father was a pastor. But even he refused to help foot the bill.

Finally, Teresa struck a deal with the students, saying, "I know you have worked hard, and it seems like I am acting unfairly. So I will let everyone in the school have a special treat – extra bread this week." The girls brightened at the thought of getting the extra bread, and they left. But still they were very disappointed.

Not long afterward, a small group of them came back. Again they tried to present their case. "We worked so hard and gave it our all. We want to go into music for a career." Teresa tried to convince them that she really was happy that these girls had the courage to try to argue with her and they had a strong point, but it just wasn't going to happen.

Again, she thought the situation was resolved. But several days later Andrew answered the door at their private quarters and told Teresa she had some more visitors. These students told her that two of the girls were so disappointed that they were physically sick. They could not eat or sleep, much less study. One of them could not stop crying. This delegation told her that the surrounding schools had assumed that JAMS would send a team to compete, and if they did not, the school would be "red marked," meaning that they would not be invited to any competitions in the future.

Teresa asked how they knew that. The girls replied that they had done some research into the situation, saying, "You always taught us to fight for what we believe." Teresa sighed, "It's not that I don't want you to go. We cannot afford it."

She sat down with the girls and showed them the math. Finally, they could see that there was simply no way the school could afford the cost of the competition – not even if they just sent their two top contenders.

In the end, the girls realized that they could not possibly win this argument. One of the most talented musicians – the daughter of the pastor - had a hard time overcoming her disappointment, and her grades went down for the next couple of months, but eventually she bounced back.

Teresa lamented, "In my heart, I really felt for her, but there really was nothing that we could do." In other schools, every family is charged

5000 shillings, the equivalent of $70 or $80 for extracurricular activities. But at JAMS three fourths of the girls cannot even afford the basic costs of tuition.

It is hoped that eventually some of the girls will be able to earn money through the microenterprises. This will provide a means for them to pay for the costs of their extracurricular competitions. But that is several years down the road.

Harold

Harold has been a fixture at the school since before it was built. He is a pleasant young man who means well and frequently offers to help. But he appears to be mildly retarded and not well coordinated. So unfortunately much of what he attempts is not handled particularly well. Nevertheless, he excels in "street smarts." He has connections throughout the nearby villages; he knows where to obtain anything; and he is willing to negotiate for whatever the school needs. In addition, he has developed a reputation as the "go to guy" for the school, so villagers often contact him first if they would like to meet with Teresa or sell something to the school.

One of Harold's jobs at the school was serving as a night watchman. But he had a different interpretation of his duties. He would be wide awake near school all day. At night, he would stay by the dormitory door. Whenever girls needed to leave, he would follow them. Naturally, the girls found this "creepy," and they complained to Teresa. But Harold protested, "Mom, these are girls, and there are no lights outside. There could be snakes in the bush. They need me there with my flashlight." Naturally, he would fall asleep at night, but he swore he would wake up at the slightest sound – though he did not hear Andrew step over him while he slept outside of the door of the main house one night!

Perhaps he might be best described as a crafty survivor. When Teresa would finish painting walls, he would steal away the empty buckets and sell them to the neighbors. When a stranger (e.g. construction workers) would approach the school, Harold was the self-appointed greeter who would – for a price – purchase and cook a chicken for them. Of course, the visitor would be surprised when Harold would eat half of the chicken he had prepared.

But the final straw came when Harold decided that he should be able to drive the school tractor. Unbeknownst to Teresa, he had convinced the driver to let him practice occasionally. And when the headmaster needed water, he had no idea that Harold was not licensed when the young man jumped into the tractor, pumped water, and brought it back up the hill. But one night Teresa was awakened when she sensed lights flickering outside of her window. She ran out and saw that Harold had disengaged the hand brake, so the tractor was slowly going backwards down the slope towards the dining room. She yelled at him, "Stop! What are you doing?" Harold replied innocently that he had been resting. So Teresa asked why the lights had been flickering, and Harold confessed that he had wanted to "take a small ride." Teresa gave him his severance pay and instructed him not to show up again.

He still comes back regularly, hoping to find work. And really, how angry can Teresa be with someone who has saved her cell number on his phone as "My Mother"!

Town / Gown Relationships

The girls who grew up in the village had foul mouths. Swearing was a natural part of their conversation. So Teresa told them, "You have home language and school language. If you feel like using a bad word, run to the gate first to calm down. But if I hear you swear, I'll give you soap to wash your mouth." Problem solved.

Gossiping was another part of village life. But the girls were learning how to solve problems before they approached Teresa, so they would say, "If you want to gossip, I won't be your friend." And soon the story-teller would have no friends.

But of course it was important to show respect for people from the town, and Teresa knew that she would need to hire adults from the town to work at the school. So she reached out to engage the locals.

One task was guarding the school. She found that she needed watchmen round-the-clock since the school is located in an area where people are extremely poor. So two watchmen were hired – one from 6 am until 6 pm and the other from 6 pm until 6 am.

One night, while the girls were enjoying a movie, someone did indeed break into one of the dorms. The dormitory had been locked, but the intruder found a crack in a glass, was able to break it further, and reached in to open the door. One girl had felt sick, and she was sleeping alone in the dorm. Fortunately, Carol had needed to return to collect something, and she encountered the thief stealing – of all things – wash basins. Carol screamed, and the burglar ran away. But where had the night watchman been? It turned out that he had left the compound to buy medicine. When he did not show up the following day and he refused to talk to the police, Teresa began to suspect that he had been "in cahoots" with the thief. So he was fired. Losing his job meant a lot to the family, since Teresa had been helping pay for his son's fees at another school.

But JAMS has had better experiences with hiring others from the neighboring community. Since some of them are farmers, they have been a tremendous help in preparing the hard ground for farming. They also helped with planting trees, loading materials, digging for underground water tanks, preparing the ponds, etc. One father of a JAMS student was paid for doing all of the roofing for the school. Part of his payment went to his daughter's fees. Another father was good at plumbing. Though the daughters of the roofer and the plumber were not outstanding students, it was still important to include children from the neighborhood at the school to maintain good relations with the neighbors and to benefit the school. This can be trying at times. Once, Teresa came upon the roofer shortly after he had planted 10 banana trees. He had assumed she would be pleased with his initiative.

When she asked why he had done it, he insisted "I wanted to do something that would help." What he apparently had not realized was that he had planted the trees in a very rocky part of the land, so there would be no room for the roots to grow when the trees got bigger. Fortunately, Teresa is familiar with banana trees, so she realized that it would be possible to take cuttings from the trees and plant them in better soil at a later date.

Although other townspeople have on occasion offered chickens to Teresa, she has learned that there may be strings attached. At first, they are trying to give her a chicken. But later they are equally likely to approach her as if she were an old friend and ask her to educate their daughter!

June

June is the oldest of 10 children. Their father is a herdsman. While he had been working at JAMS, he observed how happy the students were, and he resolved that June should be admitted.

After June had been at the school for a while, it was clear that her father was not paying her fees. Teresa approached him, saying, "I have to pay the teachers." The father protested, "I honestly don't have the money, but I will give whatever it takes." He tried to get Teresa to talk with villagers to hear their stories about how radically the girl had changed as a result of attending JAMS.

One day, Teresa was riding in a public transport van to the town, and she overheard some people talking. Apparently someone had pointed out to a friend that the van had just stopped at the road leading to JAMS. The friend replied with a story about a girl who attended the school. According to the story, when the girl had been in the eighth grade, she had a reputation for loitering. (The reputation might not have been deserved. Girls who simply walk around a shopping center are casually labeled as "prostitutes.") But since this student had been attending JAMS, she stayed at home, only venturing out to go to church, where she was very well behaved. The woman concluded, "I don't know what they do to the girls in that school."

Her companion remarked, "It must be a very expensive private school."

The woman replied, "But her father is just a herdsman."

At this point, Teresa realized that her fellow traveler had been describing June's experience, and Teresa knew that the girl had taken to heart her lectures, "If I go to town and see you walking the streets, you are accountable to me. If you are at home, then study and stay at home. Only leave to go the market, then return home immediately. " One reason Teresa gives this lecture is that the girls from JAMS are well fed. This makes them more attractive than many of the other adolescents in the town, and they become a sexual target for older men.

Indeed, one girl had been expelled from JAMS before her second year, because she had frequently been seen standing on corners in the town.

Abigail

During the first year of the school, Teresa received a call asking whether she would consider enrolling a girl named Abigail. This 15-year-old had managed to score 349 out of 500 points on the national exam, which qualified her for a provisional school, but her family could not afford to send her to one. Even more impressive was the fact that Abigail had beaten the odds. Like many of the students who are admitted to JAMS, Abigail had attended a primary school which was not considered to be strong. In addition, she had missed two out of the previous three terms because her family had lacked the funds to send her there. In retrospect, Teresa believes that Abigail would have earned at least 460 points on the national test if she had been given an adequate preparation.

The first thing Teresa noticed when she met Abigail was that the girl was extremely malnourished. She was tall, but she "looked like a string." It turned out that Abigail was in the care of her grandmother. She had no memory of her mother, who had died when Abigail was very young. Her father was paralyzed from a stray bullet which had struck him in the spine. Her grandmother was a strong woman, who was caring for six of her children's children. She was deeply committed to making sure that the children received an education, but there was no money in the household.

In order to afford the requisite books, uniforms, and tests, Abigail made and sold charcoal. This means she would chop wood into chips and pack it, topped with clay, in a bag. The wood chips would burn slowly for a week. Then they would be repacked into bags and carried to the market, where a large bag would sell for only 300 shillings ($4). She also worked for hours wading in rice paddies. During this time, leech-like slugs would cling to her legs, which became covered with scars. Food and shoes were not priorities for the struggling family.

Not having shoes would be a problem for a student at JAMS, since the school is located in a rugged terrain. So one day shortly after Abigail arrived at the school, Teresa surprised her with a pair of shoes. The girl burst into tears, because she was so overwhelmed that someone would give her something new when she had not even asked for it.

Like all of the students at JAMS, Abigail was fed a healthy diet of maize and beans. But shortly after she arrived, her legs and feet ballooned to the point that she could not walk. Teresa took her to a doctor who determined she had been so badly malnourished that a diet which was considered typical actually poisoned her system. He ordered an injection. But by then, her veins were terribly thin, and while the nurse was trying to administer the treatment Abigail screamed so loudly that Teresa was sure she was dying. Eventually, the IV was in place, and after just an hour, Abigail's body reacted so well that she remained healthy for the rest of her stay at JAMS.

When they returned to the school, Abigail became a "B+" student. Although she was fluent in Luo, her English was so underdeveloped, that she could hardly converse with others at JAMS, so she was extremely quiet. This would be a severe handicap at the school, and Teresa realized that the only way Abigail would become fluent in English would be to speak with others. So Teresa created a policy for the school. Taking a cue from Piaget, she realized that mistakes simply reflect the rules children have created to make sense of their world. The fact that they are actively trying to form these rules means they are working hard at learning. Therefore, no one should feel self-conscious about making a mistake in grammar or spelling, and everyone at the school has a duty to help others learn. This meant that anyone should feel free to correct the grammar of anyone else. In fact, students could call out a teacher's mistake – as happened when Teresa accidentally spelled "dining" with a double "n." This was one of many steps which Teresa took in creating a climate where collaboration is honored.

Beyond this step, Teresa worked directly with Abigail by giving her a set of Reader's Digest stories. For each story which she read, the girl was urged to look up unfamiliar words, write the story in her own words, and then tell the story to someone else. Abigail eagerly accepted the challenge. She did this so faithfully that by the end of her second term, she found herself at the top of the class, and from then on she never achieved less than an "A" in any subject.

In fact, her dedication benefited the school itself. Once, the students at JAMS school were participating in a district-wide math competition. Abigail's outstanding performance caught the eye of a math teacher from another school, who was amazed that a girl would be so skilled in the subject. That experience convinced him to apply to work at JAMS, because he wanted to teach in a setting where his efforts would be worthwhile – where girls were truly interested in mathematics, and he could make a difference.

What helped motivate Abigail to show such a commitment to education? Teresa credited the girl's grandmother, who insisted that she would "do anything it takes" to obtain an education for her grandchildren. There was no question that the grandmother recognized Abigail's aptitude. The older woman was convinced that if someone ever had the audacity to try to bewitch Abigail, the girl's intelligence would repel the spell, which would kill the perpetrator. The grandmother admonished Abigail not to waste her opportunity and never to complain. In fact, Teresa was instructed to tell the grandmother if Abigail ever complained.

Clearly, Abigail had taken her grandmother's words to heart. The girl spent every waking moment doing something constructive. When she was not in class or studying, she would be planting and caring for seedlings in the school's nursery. She was constantly on the alert for any way that she could show her appreciation for the opportunities she had been given. No sooner would Teresa say, "There is a mess which needs to be cleaned behind the dormitory." Abigail would take care of the problem. Eventually, Teresa learned not to mention anything that needed to be fixed when Abigail was anywhere nearby.

Two years after the girl had arrived at the school, Andrew saw that she was limping. When asked "Why?" Abigail sheepishly replied that her shoes were "a little tight." Clearly, this was an understatement. Now that she was routinely eating a healthy diet, Abigail had grown into a big girl, and she had outgrown her shoes to the point where she had cut spaces for her toes to stick out. Teresa was able to contact the girl's sponsor, who happily paid for new shoes.

In some ways, Abigail's story is typical of the students at JAMS. Many of the girls come to the school with extremely sad stories. And yet, after being there a month, they seem to have started over – they are happily looking forward, rather than dwelling on the past. The students at JAMS come from poverty. For many, this is the first time they have even seen a bed.

During the first year, Teresa invited a colleague, Dr. Teresa Fisher, to visit the school. Dr. Fisher is a professor of educational counseling. Yet even her trained eye could not readily distinguish Abigail from the other students. She concluded that the students at JAMS could be characterized as "resilient." With remarkable speed, students like Abigail have turned around their academic lives, and this gives them renewed confidence and hope for the future.

"Stop! Don't Tell Me Any More Stories!"

There is no doubt that Teresa and Andrew's lives have been turned upside down by the experience of starting JAMS. At first, they had assumed that if the effort proved to be too costly or difficult, they could easily call it quits and not look back. But then they began to meet the girls and now they have seen how many lives have been profoundly affected by the school. They wish that other people could experience the rewards they have felt.

We were meeting on an extremely snowy day in DeKalb, and Andrew noted that his shoes were not up to the task of keeping his feet dry and warm. But he was thinking twice before buying an extra pair of shoes, knowing how much is needed by people in Muhoroni. Teresa agreed that, "To a large extent, without thinking about it, our life has become extremely basic. And yet, we feel very privileged."

And with each new story they hear, their resolve is strengthened. They thought they had heard everything. No longer would they be surprised by the plight of children in rural Africa. But the stories don't stop. Teresa and Andrew knew that they only had enough money to admit a few more students for the next term. One of the applicants told the following story:

The father had been working menial jobs, when it became clear that he had contracted the AIDS virus, and he died. The family's daughter had done very well at a school run by missionaries. But now her mother could no longer afford to live in Kisumu, much less pay the 5000 shillings which she still owed the school. When the results of the 8th grade examinations came in, the girl qualified for one of the top schools. But her primary school refused to turn over the invitation letter until her family paid the amount due.

So the mother approached a member of Sango Association, saying that her daughter would not be able to attend any other reputable school without that letter, and the family had nothing – no money, no home. As if that were not enough cause for concern, now the mother had HIV, and she was getting sicker. She told Teresa, "I could die anytime." In lieu of the letter, Teresa arranged for the girl to be interviewed, and the interviewer confirmed that indeed the daughter was very smart. To give the mother at least some peace of mind, the girl was admitted in January, 2014.

This girl was part of the form 1 students admitted in January, 2014. All of the scholarship money had been allocated. But after admissions were complete, Teresa received two more calls from the headmaster, and when she heard the following desperate stories, she knew that somehow additional girls needed to be allowed to study at JAMS.

Jane was a 16-year-old orphan. She had taken her primary school exams at age 14 and passed them, but no one could pay for her to attend secondary school. She loved learning so much that she had stayed at the primary school, and eventually she took and passed the exams a second time.

Now the kind of passion which would cause a young girl to stay in primary school and take the test repeatedly is extremely rare in Kenya. Her grandmother called one of the directors of Sango and begged, "Please, this is her last chance." So when Teresa heard the story, she agreed to admit Jane to JAMS – even though she would be older than the others admitted to form 1. That night, Teresa slept soundly, knowing that she was doing all that she could to help the girl. But as soon as she woke in the morning, she received a second call.

Linda had been born out of wedlock, and she was being raised by her grandmother. Teachers at her primary school realized how bright she was, and they offered to help. So now Linda was rotating between three homes – her grandmother's, her aunt's, and her teachers'.

Unfortunately, her scores were not high enough, and she was not accepted into JAMS initially. Feeling hopeless, every morning the girl would go to the teachers' door to pray and cry. Then she would go to her grandmother's house and repeat the ritual. So her former teachers came to JAMS and pleaded with the headmaster. They told him that the girl was at the point of committing suicide, and they offered to contribute enough money to buy her uniform.

Now Teresa knew how little money primary teachers earn. She realized that most of them could not even afford to send their own children to secondary school. So this had to be an exceptional case. On top of that, she knew that she could not live with herself if something bad happened to the girl. So Linda was admitted to JAMS.

Miraculously, the school received contributions of money which covered the costs of educating one of these girls, and Teresa reasoned that they would be cooking enough food to feed 75 – what was one more mouth? But she did instruct the headmaster NOT to tell her about any more hard luck stories in the spring of 2014.

Marie

She was a beautiful girl who was referred to JAMS by one of the first teachers. Marie's mother had died four years earlier. Her father had lost his job and was in poor health. But her wealthy uncle had stepped up and paid for her to attend school. Perhaps the uncle became jealous when Marie outperformed his own child and was invited to attend a prestigious national school. For whatever reason, the uncle refused to pay any more for her education.

Recognizing how smart his daughter was, Marie's father took her to the national school and gave them his whole life savings – 8,000 shillings. If he had expected the headmaster to be sympathetic, he was sadly mistaken. The administrator told him the school would keep the money as a down payment, but now the father must return home and raise an additional 28,000 shillings in order for Marie to be admitted.

This response sent the father over the edge psychologically, and the impoverished man who had lost his job, his health, and his money, now lost his mind. Sensing that there was no hope, Marie would stay by the door to her house and cry for hours on end.

This was the situation when the teacher encountered her and brought Marie to JAMS. As soon as the girl was introduced to the school, she impressed Teresa with how healthy ("plump") she was and how much she smiled. In a now-familiar pattern, Teresa called Andrew, who approached a close friend at the university, Kurt Thurmaier, the Director of Public Administration. Kurt and Andrew had collaborated on a program in Tanzania. After consulting his wife, Kurt agreed to pay for Marie's tuition.

The minute that Teresa told Marie about her benefactors, the girl began to cry. Teresa asked her, "Why do you laugh one minute and cry the next?"

Marie hugged her and answered, "My mom died, but now I have another mom. I didn't think I'd ever call anyone 'Mom' again."

Teresa was so moved that she replied, "I'll be your mom forever!"

Thereafter, Marie worked hard and developed the best English and writing skills of any student at the school.

Teresa had hoped to meet Marie's father sometime. But he came to the school at a time when she was not there. He had brought 1000 shillings to pay as much as he could for her education. The headmaster accepted it, but later he had second thoughts. He told Teresa, "If you had seen the father, so thin and sick, you wouldn't have taken his money."

Not long afterwards, Marie's older sister found the father extremely weak at his house. He had gone for three days without food. He was taken to the hospital, where he died.

The headmaster contacted Teresa in the US, saying, "Marie is worried that she will need to leave school now that her father has died."

Teresa assured him that the girl could always stay at JAMS. She arranged for the school's matron to take Marie to the funeral and back to the school.

At this point, the rich uncle came to the school and said that he still wasn't willing to pay for her education, but she could come to his house during the break. Knowing that Marie was scared that her uncle would assume guardianship, Teresa told him that she knew he had refused to help the girl when she most needed it, and if he wasn't willing to pay the fee now, he needed to leave.

The next time Teresa saw Marie, the girl appeared to be very depressed. Teresa sat down with her and revealed that she too had lost both of her parents so she knew what it was like to be an orphan (neglecting to mention that this had happened when Teresa was an adult). "But even so, now I am helping you, and when you grow up, I expect that you will help someone else." This cheered the girl.

Then Marie's benefactor, Kurt, sent her a fleece shirt. He admitted that he had worn it once, and it probably should be washed before she put it on. But Marie refused to wash it. The shirt represented her connection to him, so she put it on and even slept in it. Kurt wrote to her, saying, "You are my godchild now."

And Teresa exclaimed, "How lucky can you be?"

Eventually, her mother's sister got in touch with the headmaster at JAMS. She said, "I don't have any money for her fees, but she can come to my home during breaks." Apparently Marie's father had kept her away from the mother's family, but now that he had died, this "mom" could connect with her niece. Marie was delighted, and has adjusted well to this new-found relationship.

When Teresa reflects on Marie's story, she comments, "I look at these kids, and know that they are dying silently. We may see a child who is running around and assume they are OK, just like Marie who often looks healthy and happy. You would never know to look at her that she was not feeling well. In fact, by the time she complains about feeling sick, you know she needs to be taken directly to the hospital."

Recognizing the role of stress in the students' lives, Teresa knew why they would frequently say that their stomachs hurt. So in 2012 she brought 1000 antacid capsules to the school. Now, when a student seems stressed, she will give them a "purple pill." This has resulted in far fewer stomach aches. Clearly, Marie has a special place in Teresa's heart, and Teresa treasures a letter which the girl wrote to her.

TO MUM & DAD:

I'm sorry I had to write a letter because I can't express my feelings in words because whenever I start my tears start rolling.

I want to thank you for what you have done to me. You have really contributed in the most important part of my life. I just don't know what words to use to express my thank you to me you.

You have do me great and all the days of my life I will live to remember you. You adm. allowed me to your school when I had lost hope of going to school, found me a sponsor, took care of me and treated me like any other person, took me to the hospital when I was sick and provided me with things I need in school.

Whenever I see you I feel like saying thank you all the time and whenever I see your eyes I lose the courage to look at them anymore. Because all the things you have done to me get written on them.

Thank you very much and hope that God will bless you even more, may you continue with the heart you have. Mum & Dad I appreciate you very much. These things will remain written in my mind, heart and soul as long as I live. Bye.

Marie's Letter

How Does JAMS Compare to a Rural Tanzanian School?

Kurt Thurmaier has formed a partnership with a secondary school in Tanzania, where he coordinates a study-abroad program for NIU students to learn about NGOs working with the Catholic church. Service Learning is a component of the NIU program, so Kurt's students helped build a dormitory at the school. But he realized that providing energy to a building in rural Tanzania would be costly, so he needed to enlist the help of an engineer who could help provide sustainable energy. Naturally, he turned to his friend Andrew, who organized an experience for his students. They worked through Engineers Without Borders to install solar panels in six classrooms.

This experience provided Andrew with an opportunity to look inside a public high school in another African nation. What he saw concerned him very much. He quickly discovered that Kenyan schools have a major advantage over Tanzanian institutions. In Tanzania, all primary education is conducted in Swahili, while in Kenya students learn English right from the start. When adolescents enter high school in Tanzania, suddenly they are expected to be fluent enough in English that they can comprehend advanced subject matter. Since the students are not conversant in English and even the teachers struggle with it, lessons are often delivered in halting English and then translated into Swahili. Certainly, at times it can be very useful to go over a concept twice. But the end result in Tanzania is that teachers spend twice as much time presenting material, and the achievement levels in all subjects are much lower.

When asked, "Aside from that major difference, how is the rural school in Kenya different from its counterpart in Tanzania?" Andrew replied, "There are so many ways."

For one thing, the Tanzanian school is located on fewer acres, yet it serves ten times the number of students – 600. Reasoning that even a second-rate education is better than none, the church does not turn away students who need an education. So they keep admitting more and more students. For instance, while Andrew was visiting, he noted that 100 students were living in a dormitory built for 60.

It is impossible to fix overcrowding quickly there. The school's administrators must wait for the government or the church to decide to allocate the money. For JAMS, Andrew and Teresa simply take out a loan and accomplish whatever needs to be done.

Because of the overcrowding, bathrooms and other parts of the Tanzanian school are "unbearably dirty." The culture at JAMS ensures that bathrooms are "clean enough that it would be possible to eat a meal there."

Further, the Tanzanian school serves both boys and girls. Although there are more girls at the school, the boys have a more spacious dormitory with more toilets.

But the most glaring difference which Andrew noted immediately was that teachers in the Tanzanian school constantly carry hardwood canes which do not break easily. These are used frequently to discipline students. Girls are caned on their hands, and boys on their bottoms. Girls often have swollen hands, which make it difficult to write. Then they are caned because their hands are swollen! This practice has convinced some students not to try. Even if they worked to complete an assignment, they might get a wrong answer, and then they would be caned – without receiving any feedback about the correct answer.

One morning, Andrew walked into a classroom while a teacher was returning students' homework. Every student was receiving two or three lashes with the cane, punishing them for mistakes. He pulled the teacher aside and told her, "I have foreign students with me, and I know that they would be traumatized if they saw caning. Please do me a favor and hold off on the caning while they are here." The teacher was not at all happy, but she realized that Andrew knew the priest in charge of the school, so grudgingly she obliged.

At JAMS, not only is no corporal punishment used, but there is a totally different relationship between the students and their teachers. Although the church manages the Tanzanian school, teachers are hired and paid by the government. They know that they will be paid, even if they do not show up to class. So they have no incentive to spend any extra time helping to ensure that students learn – unless the students have somehow managed to impress them with their intelligence. Only these students seem to have the potential of earning high scores on tests and bringing honor to the school. In contrast, at JAMS the teachers are instructed that they must help all of the students – especially the weaker ones. Teresa has assured them that the survival of the school depends on all of the students performing as well as possible. If they do not, the school will close and, of course, the teachers will be out of work.

Of course, there are other ways in which JAMS is exceptional. The professors who created the school have provided invaluable experiences for the girls to learn. For instance, when Andrew brought Engineers without Borders to JAMS school, the students were introduced to a female engineer – what a powerful role model! And when the engineers described how they were conducting research, some of the girls – Carol and Abigail – were given opportunities to help with testing the water.

Indeed, Andrew was not overstating the situation when he noted that JAMS school is different from others in Africa in "so many ways."

A School With Too Many Showers

As directors of Sango, Kim and Otieno have contact with students who have attended other schools in Kenya, and this gives them a unique perspective. They witnessed the growth of JAMS right from the start. Their first impressions of the school were "What a beautiful location on top of a hill looking over a valley." They noted that the remote hill provides more than a gorgeous view. It creates a degree of safety for the students, since it takes a real effort to reach the school.

Kim, who also serves on the Friends of JAMS Board, noted that "This is probably the first place in most of these kids' lives where they have experienced decent food, a bed, and a strong education, as well as someone who cares. The school is a godsend." When one of the other Sango students, Nancy, saw the facility at JAMS, she was amazed. She had been enrolled in a prestigious national school, and she had visited other well-regarded schools. She exclaimed, "I can't believe this is a school. It is so good." The dorms at her school were very crowded. In fact, when an inspector had visited JAMS, he had told Teresa that the school had "too many toilets and showers!"

Indeed, a lot of the high schools in Kenya are extremely large. Students do not receive individual attention from teachers, and they certainly do not benefit from guidance counselors. In fact, it appears that many secondary schools in the country have a purpose of simply identifying the select few students who might succeed in higher education. According to Otieno, those schools do not teach students to pass —"they teach them to fail." In the mid 1980's, there were so few universities that only half of one percent of the students who entered high school could hope to attend college.

But at JAMS, students receive individual attention. Many can expect to attend college. But even those who do not continue in higher education learn valuable skills which equip them to earn a living. Currently, students are learning how to tend vegetables, maintain fish ponds, and bake bread. In the future, they will be empowered to work in a dairy and to sew.

And there are important life lessons which the girls are learning, as well. Kim and Otieno have observed that students at JAMS are learning how to work together and help each other. When Sango sponsored a conference at JAMS in August, 2013, the JAMS girls routinely volunteered to clean tables, wash dishes, and assist in other ways. It was clear that they were very proud of their school. It was very difficult to get students from other schools to help out, though they were impressed with how well the school is maintained.

Kim and Otieno believe that JAMS students take ownership in their school in part because they have seen the hands-on concern of the headmaster. While other headmasters stay in their offices, the one at JAMS often works in the garden and assists in the dining room.

Polly

Agape Children's Home Ministry in Kisumu was created by a woman from America in an effort to rehabilitate street children, with the goal of reuniting them with their families. Three years ago, the ministry began to serve girls. Polly was in the first group of girls. She was an orphan who had lived for a while with her aunt. But reuniting her with that family member was out of the question – her aunt had been the one who had prostituted her and subjected her to child labor. Polly had run away from her aunt's house, but there was nowhere for her to go, so she got caught again in the street culture.

So Agape had rescued her and had given her a primary education. By then, they determined that she could live with her brother and sister in Nairobi. They would be responsible for ensuring that her education continued. But Lisa, a representative of Agape followed up after Polly had taken her exams, only to find that she had scored a pitiful 169 points out of 500. She certainly was not prepared for secondary school.

Lisa was amazed. She had held high hopes for Polly. She had lived with Polly for a while and knew her to be extremely hard-working, dedicated, and a very good person. So why had she performed so poorly on the tests? It turned out that – instead of letting Polly study for the exam, her sister had kept her at home, caring for young children. Lisa could not stand by and watch society fail this young girl. She called Otieno and explained the situation, saying, "The only place we can take her would be JAMS. Please help me." Otieno protested that Sango had a firm rule that prevented them from giving a scholarship to a student with such a low score, but he encouraged Lisa to contact Teresa.

A complicating factor was that by now Polly was 18 years old. But Teresa had seen one such older student succeed at another school and go on to a university. So Teresa agreed to let Polly attend the school if Lisa would agree to pay extra for the tutoring that would be required to give the remedial training the girl needed. Buoyed by this hope, Lisa contacted Polly's sister to tell her the good news. But the sister retorted, "No. She failed the exam. Why waste money on her?"

Lisa was crestfallen. She turned to Teresa, asking, "What do I do now?" Now Teresa knew that Lisa needed to be secretive about the money she was promising to pay for Polly's education. Agape did not allow their employees to get involved in that way. Since Polly was 18, Teresa urged Lisa to tell the sister that Polly would get a job at JAMS. She would be an employee in the kitchen. Apparently the sister assumed she would benefit from Polly's salary, and she agreed to release the girl.

And so, Polly was admitted to JAMS, but she brought absolutely nothing with her. Teresa was not concerned about this. Since the school routinely provides uniforms and hygienic supplies, those needs were covered. She did instruct the headmaster to purchase some shoes for Polly. In turn, Lisa was so grateful that she repeatedly called Teresa to thank her.

So Teresa has occasionally found that she needed to make exceptions to the admission standards. But she has decided not to take girls whose stories have been exposed in the country's newspapers. One of these sensationalized stories described a 15-year-old whose father died when she was seven years old. Her mother got her circumcised and announced, "Now you are an adult, and you can get married." This would provide a way for the mother to get some free cows, as the girl's dowry. Fortunately, the government heard about the situation, retrieved her, and sent her to a boarding school. When the girl was 12 years old, her mother was bit by a dog and died from rabies.

Despite this horrific history, the girl had scored well on her high school entrance exam – 389 points. But Teresa resisted admitting the girl to JAMS. She knew that people from throughout the world would contribute money for her education as soon as they had heard the girl's sad story. In contrast, most of the girls at JAMS were likely to be overlooked and forgotten by the wider community. They were more likely to fall through society's cracks.

The Games Parents Play

When cousins Patricia and Lucy walked to their primary school, they watched as JAMS was being built, and they saw the first class of students come to the school. So when they were in the eighth grade, one told her father that she wanted to check out the school. He brought the girls, and they found Teresa, who gave them a snack. For two hours, the girls played while Teresa talked with the father. By then it was 4 pm, and the father told the girls they needed to leave before it got too dark. For the next hour, the girls disappeared from sight. Finally at 5 pm the father insisted that they really needed to go.

Teresa asked how far away they lived. Knowing that it would be easier for the father to walk them home in the morning, she asked the girls if they would like to stay for the night. They readily agreed. The next day, when Teresa called the father, he said that he was really busy, but the girls could return home on their own.

After the girls took their high school entrance exams, the father returned to Teresa to tell her that they had performed quite well, and his brother and he had agreed that Patricia and Lucy could apply to JAMS. They were admitted in the second class of students.

The girls were a good influence on each other. They chose to sleep on the top bunks of neighboring beds. One was brighter, but she was able to challenge her cousin to perform better.

After the cousins had been at JAMS for a year, Teresa received a call from Patricia's father who asked, "What are you doing to these kids?"

Teresa took a deep breath and prepared herself for the worst, but the father continued, "Patricia is so much more responsible than her older sister." As soon as she came home for a break, she announced that the house was too dirty. At school, she had learned that even the bathroom needs to be clean enough for someone to be willing to eat there. Now she set to work cleaning and rearranging the furniture at home, and she was even instructing her family about how to eat healthy meals.

It was clear that the girls really loved being at the school. Unfortunately, their fathers were farmers, and their crops had suffered from droughts. So they struggled to pay the fees. Girls like Lucy and Patricia who come from very poor families take great pride in their academic achievement. So Teresa had resolved to be flexible. But two years passed with no fees paid.

Now the public schools in Kenya are very inflexible, so if a parent misses one payment, the administrator sends the child home. It turned out that the cousins had siblings in public schools, and since JAMS school seemed to be more willing to negotiate when they were paid, the fathers had been prioritizing paying the public schools.

So finally, after two years, Teresa told the girls they must leave the school and return home. Lucy hid in the bathroom. When the headmaster found her there, she was huddled by a wall and crying, "Please. I don't want to go home." The headmaster called Teresa, who contacted the girl's father. Low and behold, by the end of the day, he had brought some money.

Patricia did return home, but she was concerned that her father might send her to a different school. Apparently some parents try to game the system – if they are fortunate enough to find a school which tolerates late payments, they wait until the school loses patience. Then they enroll their child in another school and play the same game. But Patricia insisted she would not go to another school, and her father understood what an effect JAMS had had on her.

So Patricia's father came to Teresa and explained that he had not been paid by a coffee processor for the beans which he had delivered two months earlier. Nevertheless, he was confident that he would be paid in two weeks. Teresa told him that he should have come earlier to explain the situation. But she knew from previous experience that when another farmer had finally received his money, he had conveniently forgotten to pay the fees. So she instructed the headmaster that if the money did not come in two weeks, the girl must be sent home to remind her father of his obligation.

Now that Teresa has learned about the games parents play, she insists that they make a minimum down payment before a girl who is not on scholarship can be admitted.

"You're Spending So Much Energy, But You're Not Working Hard!"

Diana was one of the first fundraisers for the school as well as the first president of the Friends of JAMS foundation. She found that air travel would cost $2000, and she debated whether it would be a wiser use of her funds simply to donate that money to JAMS, rather than making the trek to the school. Teresa replied, "No. Come and see the school first. You need that experience when you ask others to contribute."

It turned out that Diana had lived in South Africa when she was young, so she felt comfortable with the idea of traveling alone to rural Kenya. Her biggest hurdle came when she went to a health clinic and was given a long list of required immunizations. Furthermore, even those would not be sufficient to protect her if she did not wash her hands repeatedly when she got to the school.

Nevertheless, she vowed to visit the school. Teresa is pretty sure that the condition of the school was more primitive than Diana had expected. At that time, they had no solar-powered electricity. In fact, the dining hall/kitchen had not yet been constructed. A temporary shack made of wood and iron sheets housed the fire for cooking. And there was no sink for washing utensils – much less running water.

Diana is a professor of English at Northern Illinois University, so she had much to offer the girls, who were trying to master the language. As soon as she arrived, Diana began sitting down with the students and chatting with them. She found that many of them were sharing heart-breaking stories. Teresa recalled, "I can't tell you how many times Diana cried when she was just listening to their stories. Then she would come to me and ask, 'Did you know....?'" Teresa assured her that she had already done her crying. Now she was just trying to do her best to help the girls.

Diana had hoped to work with the girls to perfect their English writing, but she discovered that their language skills were not developed enough to begin writing. So she focused on communicating with them orally. She told them about everyday experiences at her kitchen table, and she shared stories and pictures of her dog, Tilly.

The girls were surprised to hear Diana's stories. Why would anyone have a table in their kitchen? And dogs in Kenya were used solely for security, while cats were mousers. It seemed weird that this American professor would actually love her dog!

Next, Diana went to the building created for the library. Donated books were still in boxes, and she began to sort them. While she was organizing the library, she encountered several jigsaw puzzles. She opened one and began working on it. Soon she found herself surrounded by students who had never seen such a puzzle before. Diana showed them how to piece it together. The girls were so excited that they did not want to stop when it became dark. So they lit lanterns, and they did not go to bed until the paraffin in the lanterns ran out. Even then, some of the girls got up at 5 am the next morning so that they could work on the puzzle for an hour before the day began.

From then on, Teresa has made it a point to bring jigsaw puzzles with her. The girls compete to put them together. Assembling these puzzles has become a favorite pastime, particularly for girls in form 1 when they enter the school.

Diana also introduced the girls to binoculars. The girls would join her in looking for and identifying birds. When she returned to the US, the glasses remained at the school, and some of the students have really taken to bird-watching.

On Saturdays, the girls till the ground to weed the school farm. The soil is rich and black, but during the dry season it becomes extremely hard. The students use hoes with rounded metal disks at the end of a handle. Girls from farms are experts at digging into the soil. But when Diana tried to strike the hard ground with a hoe, she couldn't even make a dent. One of the girls told her, "You're spending so much energy, but you're not working hard!!" They tried unsuccessfully to show her the proper technique.

Diana's experience was similar to that of girls who came from nearby "cities" (small towns, by American standards). These students had come from families with white-collar jobs. Some of them had fathers who were clerks. Like Diana, they were amazed at how easy tilling the ground seemed to be for the rural girls. This was a good lesson for the city girls, who grew to admire the expertise of the rural students. One of these girls, Melissa, exclaimed, "I can't imagine how they do it – they even sing while they are working!" Melissa was determined to perfect the skill, and she would practice alone in the field until she became quite good. In turn, the girls who had grown up on farms realized they could feel pride in their ability to work the land.

The rural students were also talented at identifying plants which could be used to treat stomach aches and other ailments. Ellen developed a reputation for her ability to treat sprained muscles. She would pound leaves and mix them with petroleum jelly to create a soothing muscle-relaxant which she massaged into the affected area.

Unfortunately, the students' knowledge of plants did not include carrots. Teresa taught the first girls how to plant carrots in mounds of soil. And yet, those vegetables stubbornly refused to grow. Eventually, Teresa investigated further, and discovered that the girls were carefully weeding the garden. But apparently the leaves of carrots were very similar to leaves on a nearby tree, so they had assumed that they were ridding the garden of pesky weeds, when in fact they had been discarding young carrot plants!

Three Meals a Day

While Diana was visiting JAMS during the first summer, it was time to harvest the corn. In order to do this, stalks were cut and assembled like "teepees" to dry. They were left that way for two weeks. At which time, the ears of corn were picked and the stalks were left in the fields. The corn was dried some more. This was an onerous task. Each morning, the ears of corn were spread on a concrete veranda, which absorbed the sun and helped to speed the drying process; then at night, all of the corn needed to be taken inside to protect it from rain or early morning dew.

After the "maize" was sufficiently dried, the girls would use a knife to remove one row of kernels. Then they would use their fingers to flick off the rest. Often, they would develop blisters from working with the hard, dry kernels. Bags of kernels would be taken to a mill, which ground the maize into flour. This flour would be cooked in boiling water until it reached the consistency of grits. This is known as "ugali." At first, Diana did not enjoy eating ugali, but in those early days, three quarters of the diet at the school consisted of ugali and kale. Meat was only served once a week, and Teresa was adamant that all adults would eat the same food as the students were served. The diet at JAMS is high in carbohydrates, but that works well for the students.

Teresa's uncle, who is a doctor, had advised her to try to work millet into the girls' nutrition, since it is rich in iron, and it would help them develop immunity for many diseases. So, even though millet is expensive, a typical breakfast at the school consists of porridge made from ground corn, millet, and cassava (cassava is the starch that people spray on clothes during ironing to stiffen them).

At 11:00, the girls get a break for tea and bread.

At 1:30, lunch might include rice and lentils or ugali and kale or rice and sossy (a soy-bean produce which has the consistency of meat but can be purchased for $1/8^{th}$ of the cost).

Dinner is at 6:30. Typically, this meal consists of rice and sossy, or beans and maize, or chapatti (a flat bread like a tortilla) served with lentils, or ugali and kale. A favorite dish, which the girls call "egg stew" is served for Friday dinner. Teresa created the recipe as a special treat for the end of the week. It consists of hard-boiled eggs mixed with onions, tomatoes, other vegetables, and spices.

Three meals a day is more food than most of the girls had ever experienced before coming to JAMS. When students first arrive, they tend to stuff themselves. They eat until it looks as if they cannot breathe. At first, the cook protested that they were eating too much, but Teresa convinced her to be patient. At home, the girls had learned that the food supply could easily be exhausted, and they were afraid that before long they would go hungry. Typically, by the third week the students are reassured, and they begin to show restraint.

As Teresa has exclaimed, feeding 75 people three times a day is no joke! Each week, people at JAMS school need 1½ large bags of maize, 50 kg. of pinto beans, 50 kg. of rice (grown in a swamp not far from the school) and 10 kg. of lentils. Lentils are shipped from China. The rest is grown in Kenya.

The beans and maize grown at the school supplement food contributed by students' families. Frequently, parents of impoverished girls pay fees by giving crops to the school. Teresa has learned to make arrangements ahead of time so that when the parents harvest, they know that they owe the school 10 sacks of corn or beans, and JAMS will purchase another five from them. These sacks of food have a shelf life of three months. Crops harvested in July and August last through

December, and food harvested in January and February is sufficient to feed people at the school through April. But during May and June, local food is hard to find, and the school needs to purchase corn and beans from the market. Several times a year, Teresa buys food in bulk – in December, May, and August. In other schools, it is well known that principals skim money from the top of the food budget. Teresa has found that she can spend one third of the amount that other schools allocate for food. Unfortunately, the market's food is full of preservatives which cannot be removed.

"Do Not Turn Off Your Phone!"

Twice, in the earliest days of the school, Teresa felt scared to death. Both times, there were serious health crises.

One day, she received a call from a nearby headmaster. A doctor from the Ministry of Health had just visited his school to oversee a USAID sponsored program spraying the dormitories for mosquitoes. Now JAMS was nowhere near a body of water where mosquitos might breed, and no one had lived on the land for years, so in reality, the school had no mosquito problem. Yes, occasionally, a girl who came to the school from a coastal region would be infected with malaria, but the staff learned that the disease could readily be treated by taking that person to the hospital, and since the students used mosquito netting to surround their beds, there was no danger that they would be infected.

Nevertheless, this delegation from the government had a job to do, and they would be angry if Teresa prevented them from doing it. They were being paid for disinfecting dormitories, and they needed to prove that they were working. So Teresa told them that they were welcome to come, and the next hour was spent dragging mattresses and all of the girls' belongings out of the dormitory, so only the metal bunk bed frames remained inside the four walls.

The workers were a sight to behold. They wore uniforms that resembled Hazmat outfits, so it was clear that the spray would be dangerous. The doctor stayed just long enough to get them started with the process, then he left, with instructions that none of the students could enter the dormitory for four hours after spraying was completed.

No one was about to take those orders lightly, so they waited for four hours before they took everything back into the dorm and prepared to go to bed. An hour later, one girl after another began to itch. Some complained that their eyes were swelling shut. Others started to develop welts. Fortunately, Teresa had the doctor's phone number, and she called him. He asked whether the girls had touched the bed frames. Teresa said "You told me that you were only spraying the corners and the walls! What do I do now?" The doctor asked if she had an anti-histamine, piriton, which she could administer. Teresa made the doctor promise that he would leave his phone turned on in case she needed to call him again that night. Then she checked on the school's medical supplies. Fortunately, she had just enough piriton to give to the ones who were most severely affected. Of course, the school had no electricity, so it was pitch black in the dormitory, and Teresa needed to use a flash light to check on the girls.

After she had dispensed the medicine, some of the girls fell asleep and others were crying themselves to sleep. Teresa had a minute to breathe, and she called the neighboring headmaster to ask if his students had experienced such serious reactions to the spraying. He said that no one had complained at his school, and Teresa asked if he had <u>ever</u> seen such an outbreak. He speculated that perhaps the Health Ministry workers had begun to run low on the ingredients for the spray after they had left his school, and they might have mixed the wrong proportions. He agreed with the doctor that piriton should be the most effective treatment, and he too promised to keep his phone on "just in case."

All that Teresa could think about was what would happen if they needed to take anyone to the hospital. They had no car. All they had was a tractor with no shock absorbers. It would take at least an hour over deeply-rutted ground to reach the hospital, which was 15 miles away. In addition, it was autumn, and the temperatures of 50-60 degrees F were uncomfortably cold for the girls.

Early the next morning, Teresa called the doctor and told him that he really needed to come to the school to see how badly the spray had affected the girls. To this day, he still has not returned to JAMS.

Several months later came the second scare. Melissa, the city girl who had been so impressed by the agricultural skills of the rural girls, did not want the others to know how difficult it was for her to learn gardening. So she rarely talked to the others about what she was doing. Late one afternoon, she became distressed when she noticed some insects were attacking the plants, but she knew that she could hoist a pesticide pump on her back and carry it into the fields to take care of the problem.

The next morning, the cooks realized that they needed some kale, so they harvested it and prepared the noon meal. Later that day, the girls came together to study between 7 and 9 pm. Shortly after they had gathered, one announced that her stomach was beginning to give her problems. Then another, and another, and soon all twelve were vomiting. No one knew what was wrong. They called the headmistress, who told them to begin drinking water. Then they called Teresa who was at a university 40 miles away. She asked what they had been eating. But they assured her that they had just had vegetables, which were a normal part of their diet. All of a sudden, one girl remembered that she had seen Melissa carrying the pesticide pump out to the garden, and asked whether she had sprayed the kale. Melissa protested, "Yes. Insects were all over the plants!" But apparently she had not realized that no one was supposed to eat the kale for three days after it had been sprayed, and that the cooks must be told whenever pesticide was applied to the plants. The girls drank water all night, and eventually they began to feel better.

By then, Teresa had grown to dread unexpected calls which came from the school. But for the most part, the girls have remained very healthy. Teresa wants to believe that her uncle can take some of the credit when he recommended that they incorporate millet into the diets to strengthen the girls' immunity.

But one additional thing that distinguishes JAMS from other boarding schools in the country is the number of girls who are allowed to sleep in a dormitory. While other schools have 80 students sleeping in close quarters in a room filled with three-tier bunk beds, Teresa has limited the dorm capacity to 40 girls, sleeping on traditional bunks. It is possible that diseases do not spread quickly at JAMS because the dorms are not as congested.

Medical Adventures

With the help of her uncle, Teresa has been able to prevent many health problems. Whenever the girls return from a vacation, one of the first tasks is to "de-worm" them since they have been drinking river water and eating food directly from the soil. In addition, including millet daily in their diets, using mosquito netting, and providing ample supplies of maize are practices at JAMS which have contributed to the fact that rarely do the girls need to turn to a nearby public dispensary. At other schools, it is not unheard of for 50 students to show up at the dispensary each day.

But occasionally there are emergencies for which it would help to have a complete medical history. Unfortunately, obtaining accurate histories for the girls has not been easy. People are not willing to disclose problems that could prevent a girl from being admitted to the school. Here are two stories of girls who entered the school with serious but undisclosed health concerns.

Kathy loved to dance. When Teresa was in high school, one of the activities that she had enjoyed the most was a weekly dance. Not only was it fun, but it was a great way to release stress from studying. So there was no question that there would be chances to dance at JAMS, and this has proven to be very popular with the students.

When the girls returned to school in January, 2014, after a holiday, they were looking forward to the Friday dance. Kathy was so excited to get there that she took off running. Somehow, she slipped and fell on some concrete, and lost consciousness. This happened while Teresa and

Andrew had returned to the States, so the matron took the girl in a cab to the closest hospital. She was told that they were not equipped for a problem this serious, so they tried the next hospital, where they were given the same story. Finally, they arrived at a major hospital in Kisumu where Teresa's aunt had arranged to meet them. Now the aunt is a banker who had been planning to travel to open a new branch, and she had withdrawn money that she would need for her trip. So when they reached the hospital, she could guarantee payment for services. Otherwise, the doctors would not have touched the unconscious girl.

Teresa's aunt stayed by the girl's side, and eventually, in about ten hours, she began to move. As soon as that happened, the aunt called Teresa to tell her what was happening. Throughout the weekend Teresa was on pins and needles waiting for updates, and the telephone service seemed to be particularly uncooperative. Finally, at 6:30 Sunday morning, the aunt called Teresa, but before she could say a word, they were disconnected, and they could not reconnect the call. Teresa was frantic with worry, and immediately called the headmaster at JAMS to see whether he knew anything. To her surprise, he reported that everything was fine, and the girl was already back in school.

Fortunately, Teresa's doctor uncle had made sure that a cat scan had been performed, and he determined that the girl had no more than a nasty bump on the outside of her head. So miraculously, the fall had not been so bad. Yet why had it rendered her unconscious? The headmaster had called the girl's aunt, who had raised her. At home, dancing had been discouraged by a culture which viewed dancers as bad girls who did not work hard. It turned out that twice before, when the girl had become excited, she had passed out – apparently from anxiety attacks. The aunt had not disclosed this previously. And dancing was one thing that the girl found truly, overwhelmingly, exciting.

Now there is a major difference between government schools and private schools. Teresa's uncle told her that students in government schools are frequently beaten, and occasionally some have died from the mistreatment, with no repercussion for the school. If a student in a government school needs medical treatment, they are simply taken to the nearest dispensary, where their parents meet them and take them to the hospital.

In Teresa's private school, many of the girls are orphans, and the vast majority of parents have no money for hospital care. In fact, ¾ of the parents of girls at JAMS cannot get insurance, since they are farmers, and the government does not consider farming to be a career. Furthermore, if JAMS were found negligent in a student's death, Teresa could be imprisoned.

Polly also had an undisclosed medical condition. One day Andrew noticed that Polly appeared to have a serious limp. He asked her what was wrong, and she confessed that she had a wound on her thigh. In fact, the wound had become so deep that it was possible to see her bone. Once again, Teresa turned to her uncle. He diagnosed the problem as osteomyelitis, and clearly the girl would need an operation. Non life-threatening operations are scheduled three times a year when a team of doctors visits the region, so they made sure the girl would be seen by those doctors.

In the meantime, Teresa contacted Polly's mother. It turned out the girl had experienced pain in her leg for a number of years. When she had been five, Polly had had a boil on her thigh, and she had been taken to a hospital. They took X-rays and said it was essential that she see a doctor. But at the same time, Polly's father died, and her mother was so deeply affected by his death that she never found the time to take her daughter for the needed medical treatment. Instead, the mother tried to treat Polly's leg with traditional herbs.

In August of 2013, the team of doctors visited the area, and Brent

Wholeben, a colleague of Teresa's, volunteered to pay for Polly's treatment. It turned out that the bone had been so infected the doctors needed to cut ¼ of the way through the bone, and Polly had to remain at the hospital for a week. Unfortunately, some of the infection remained in her bone, and through the fall this spread to her flesh. So a second operation would be needed during the December break.

When the break began, early in December, Polly said that she really did not want to go home, knowing that her mother would simply insist that she take a lot of herbs. So with her mother's permission she was allowed to remain at JAMS, and on December 2nd Teresa's aunt took her back to the hospital to see a new team of doctors who were planning to remove more bone. When Teresa returned to Kenya in the middle of December, she immediately went to the hospital to visit Polly. She was surprised to find that Polly's mother had taken the girl home, where the wound had begun to bleed and the dressing had not been changed. Again, Polly was readmitted to the hospital, and this time the operation was more successful. The hospital is run by a Catholic mission, and the local Bishop is the brother of Teresa's uncle, who is a doctor at the hospital. So the Bishop trusted his brother when he guaranteed that JAMS would pay the bill. Polly's mother gave them all that she could, 200 shillings, which is equivalent to $2.50, and she was told, "If you can find it in your heart to repay the school over time, that would be fine."

Hesbon

Hesbon and Teresa had grown up together, though he was a few years older than she. Their parents had attended the same Christian church. He went on to become a banker in Nairobi for a number of years, and she became a professor in the U.S.

So she had not seen him for 20 years when Teresa encountered Hesbon at her father's funeral in 2004. But he looked much different than she had remembered. It appeared that life had really beaten him down. Apparently he had owned a van transport company, but one van had been destroyed in an accident, and one thing led to another and ultimately he had lost everything. So he had moved back to Muhoroni, and now he was farming sugar cane and raising five children. He was known in the town as being good-hearted and generous, and he was actively involved in his church.

Four years later, when Teresa was conducting her feasibility study for the school, she remembered Hesbon and wondered if he might be interested in helping out. She asked around town if anyone knew where Hesbon lived. A young boy on a motorbike told her he did, and he could take her there. So Teresa hopped on the back of his bike and bumped along the rough road to a small hut.

Hesbon was amazed to see her. He listened to Teresa's dream of starting a school. She explained that she knew she would need someone to help her. To her surprise, Hesbon replied, "I was once an employee. I'm never going to work for someone else again. But I'll help in any way that I can for free."

He had a lot of wisdom to offer her in the process. In addition to his expertise as a banker, he had chaired the board of a primary school, and had been instrumental in helping build it. So he was able to warn her about possible pitfalls – how she might be cheated by vendors and construction workers. They began chatting a couple times each week about plans for the school.

But suddenly Hesbon fell very ill with food poisoning. Apparently he had become dehydrated, and he was extremely weak. In this condition, he had collapsed. His wife discovered him at 4 in the morning, lying helpless on the ground, unprotected from the 40° F cold night air, and she took him to the hospital. He knew that his wife needed to remain at home with their youngest child, so he asked her to contact Teresa to visit him. Teresa did not know what to expect when she arrived at the hospital. She stayed with Hesbon while the hospital personnel worked to try to find a vein that had not collapsed in order to administer an IV with fluids. But he was still going to need to remain at the hospital for 3 days.

So Teresa settled in and looked around for ways she could be useful. She could not help but notice that there were no sheets or blankets on his hospital bed, so she purchased some. Unfortunately, the staff seemed to have no time to clean the linens, so Teresa washed them herself. Knowing how destitute Hesbon's family was, Teresa paid for his hospital bill. Now apparently this all caused quite a stir, and soon rumors were flying that Hesbon must have two wives – even though he seemed to be a very staunch Christian. Where had he been hiding Teresa?

His wife had had her doubts, as well, but Hesbon's aunt told her, "You should count this as a blessing. Teresa is married and does not need anything." And Teresa echoed, "I don't want to cause any problems. You called me, and I did whatever I could for someone I've known for a long time. Besides, I'm only going to be here for one or two more months this summer, then I'll be gone. So his wife and the rest of his family developed a strong respect for all that Teresa had done.

In 2009, when she was ready to begin work on the school, she contacted Hesbon and told him that she could really use his help. She would not need him to be at the school constantly, but with his expertise in money management and construction, he would be a tremendous asset to her brother James, who would do the actual work. This arrangement worked very well until James suddenly died in the tragic accident. Hesbon was deeply affected by the loss.

At that time, Teresa could not imagine how work could continue without James. But Hesbon had insisted, "This is not the time to give up. James worked so hard." And again he offered to help in any way that he could – but still on the same terms – no payment. And so, Hesbon took over managing the construction. With his knowledge of construction costs, at times he would refuse to commit the school to hiring someone to provide a service, and he would do the work himself.

Why was he so willing to do all this? Growing sugar cane is highly dependent on the seasons, so for much of the year, there is little that needs to be done. In addition, Hesbon may have felt guilty that his family was enduring such poverty following years of relative wealth. This had been particularly hard on his children. During 2010, one of Teresa's colleagues from Northern Illinois University, Lee Shumow, visited the construction site and met Hesbon, who invited her to his home. His daughter, who was in the eighth grade, proudly recited a poem to their visitor. In turn, Lee promised the girl that if she did well in school, the Shumows would pay her fees throughout high school at JAMS.

Now Hesbon lived 15 miles away from the school. So every day, he would wake up at 3 am, work until 6 on his farm, take his youngest daughter to school, walk a mile to the bus, then walk another mile and a half from the bus stop to JAMS, arriving at 10 in the morning. He would work until 5 pm and return home at 8. And for all of that, he refused to be paid.

Eventually, he even assumed increased responsibilities. When a head teacher proved to have horrible financial skills, Hesbon stepped in and offered to become the school's accountant, arranging for all purchases. Teresa agreed, on condition that he would accept at least a minimal payment - enough that she could provide health care for him. She was concerned about his health because he worked so very hard in the extreme Kenyan weather. If the tractor got stuck in mud, Hesbon would stay with it until it was freed. And he thought nothing of walking five miles in a downpour during the rainy season.

At first, Hesbon would not agree to the arrangement, but finally Teresa convinced him by saying, "I'll at least give you minimum wage so that you can get insurance. If you do not want the money, put it in the school account for your daughter. "

So now Hesbon's life has changed, his health has improved, and his outlook on life is much better. In fact, Andrew and Hesbon have become the best of friends. And both of them defer to Teresa's ability to get workers to perform their best.

"The Boss is Coming!"

Once, when Teresa was in Tanzania, Andrew and Hesbon were at JAMS with some construction workers. Teresa was surprised when Andrew called her, saying "These construction people aren't working!" It turned out that Hesbon had backed off when Andrew had shown up, and neither of them was taking responsibility for communicating with the builder. So Teresa agreed to return to Kenya. Andrew and Hesbon joked, "The Boss is coming!"

Teresa admonished the builder, saying that apparently the job had been too much for his workers, so they could only work on one of the dorms, while she would hire another crew to construct the other one. They tried to protest that she could not do that, but she assured them that she certainly could. In addition, the management responsibilities were clearly divided, with Andrew overseeing one building and Hesbon in charge of the other.

Andrew was amazed at how hard the crews began to work, and he told Teresa that they were even competing for cement. She made sure that Hesbon ordered more cement, and the construction proceeded relatively smoothly. Though of course there were occasional glitches. When that happened, Hesbon would call Andrew and say, "Something has happened, but don't tell 'Mama' until we've talked it out first!"

One day, a load of bad stones was brought to the school. Andrew mildly protested, "Don't do that!" But Teresa, who was quickly becoming a no-nonsense business woman, insisted that the firm remove the stones and deliver good ones.

Her reputation was confirmed when a brick supplier tried to short-change her – delivering 400 instead of the 600 she had purchased. She discovered that the supplier had stacked the bricks in layers in a tractor trailer, but the bricks in the lowest level were spread out, while the ones on top were tightly fitted. The supplier had counted the bricks in the top layer and multiplied by the number of levels. She assured them that they would not get away with that, and she would count every brick in the load. The driver tried to dissuade her by throwing dust at her, hoping she would give up. But Teresa challenged him, saying, "Do you see how I'm dressed? I don't mind getting dirty."

So it will be no surprise when Teresa discovered a crack in some timber that she refused to pay for it. Eventually, the supplier realized that it would be a lot easier to give her good quality lumber the first time, rather than upsetting her.

The fact that Teresa has made so many of the decisions was surprising at first to the townspeople. Apparently it is an unwritten convention in Kenya that the men defer to their wives, but people do not openly acknowledge how strong women truly are in the society. The people in the town wondered where her husband was while Teresa was laying the initial groundwork for the school. And so, in 2010, when Andrew first arrived in the town, everyone came to him to ask questions about the school. Andrew would ask them, "Have you seen me do anything around here yet? You need to go to her!"

Here was another sophisticated professor who confounded the locals when he dug in and worked hard with his hands. A friend advised him, "You shouldn't be driving a tractor. You're educated. You have money, why don't you pay other people?" Eventually their friends and neighbors grew to understand Andrew's humility and to recognize that he was a great role model who was dedicated to the cause.

Now when Andrew goes to town to buy items for the school, all he has to say is, "I'm married to Mama." And the merchants are sure to give him good quality supplies.

"Who is in Charge Here?"

Frequently, people have struggled to try to define Andrew and Teresa. They defy expectations. For instance, it surprises many in rural Kenya that Teresa and Andrew have so many friends who are white and well-educated. Among these friends, one of Andrew's students was particularly puzzling. He was a white man with long hair who was installing solar panels at a school in Tanzania.

One reason people do not expect Teresa and Andrew to be so worldly is that they dress humbly, since much of their time in Kenya is spent doing physical work. Andrew often wears torn jeans or shorts, prompting one student to ask, "Don't you have better clothes?" So a man who was delivering building materials approached one of the students and said, "Tell the guard (pointing to Andrew) to open the gate." Another time, Andrew approached a prospective Swahili teacher who was coming to interview. Andrew asked if he could help. She simply passed by him and asked a student where she could find the director. The student pointed at Andrew. The woman returned to Andrew, looking very confused and a little guilty. Andrew took her to meet with Teresa.

One time a plumber came to JAMS, and the headmaster directed him to find Teresa. The plumber made a point of ignoring the slender woman who was dressed simply. Instead, he persisted in asking one person after another, "I am looking for the owner of the school. Where can I find her?" Finally, after the job was complete and Teresa was paying him, the plumber apologized, explaining, "I expected to see a fat woman who was well-dressed, with high heels."

But having a woman as one of the school's administrators effectively plays on other Kenyan expectations, as well. Men feel comfortable bargaining prices and terms of employment with other men, but they consider it beneath them to argue with a woman. This gives Teresa an advantage. Workers have quoted outrageous rates to Andrew, but Teresa can name her own price and expect men to agree without a fight.

Once, a man who was hauling stones tried to convince Andrew and Hesbon to give him a down payment. Knowing that Teresa had refused to do so, Hesbon exclaimed, "You want us to go behind her back?!" And Andrew assured the trucker, "We have to ask her first." That ended the conversation.

JAMS School

Tractor Stories

Whenever Andrew would go to the school in the early years, much of his time was spent installing solar panels. When he was not doing that, he would be hauling supplies for the school. As soon as girls new to the school saw him heading for the tractor, they would offer to help "Daddy." Partly because they enjoyed being with him, but truth be told, also because many of them had never ridden in a motor vehicle, much less seen a tractor.

Naturally, some of Andrew's stories concern tractors. Like the time when he was pulling an old trailer behind the school's tractor. He heard a strange noise, put on the brakes, and looked down – only to see a wheel from the trailer go sailing past the tractor's cab. Or the time when the trailer hitch broke, and the trailer was left far behind while Andrew drove on.

Corrupt police figure prominently in many of the tractor stories. At first, the local police did not know what to make of it when they saw Andrew pulling a 40-year-old trailer behind a new tractor. They did not know him, and they speculated that this plainly-dressed man owned the trailer, but surely he had stolen the shiny tractor. As is the custom, the police tried to get this stranger to pay them off with a hefty bribe - $50. Fortunately, the police knew that Hesbon worked for JAMS, so when Andrew was able to call him to explain the situation, they were reassured by a familiar face. Hesbon was only expected to pay a $1 bribe!

Another time, while Andrew was hauling building materials, he was stopped by people collecting taxes on commercial vehicles. Since they did not recognize him, they refused to believe he was helping the school – until once again Hesbon came to the rescue.

Teresa has had her share of misadventures while driving the tractor, as well. Even though the vehicle had legitimate license plates, police who stopped her insisted that the tags were not genuine, and since the tractor might be stolen, they should confiscate it. Teresa knew that they expected a bribe. At first, the police were threatening her with a 1000 shilling "fine," but eventually they realized that she really did own this nice tractor, so clearly she must be wealthy – and the amount skyrocketed to 3000 shillings. Naturally, Teresa called Hesbon.

Since then, Teresa and Andrew have worked to keep their good relationship with the local authorities. Once, when they saw a police man in a local pub, Teresa offered to buy him a drink. Only when it came time to pay did she realize that he had ordered a whole bottle of whiskey on her tab.

The good news is that now when the police see the JAMS tractor, they recognize it. So the driver always carries a dollar to pay their "fee."

A Penny for Your Thoughts

Two stories represent problems that arose when adults did not try to communicate with Teresa. The first concerns a parent, and the second involves a teacher.

One girl had left after the first year. Hesbon knew the mother, so he was able to tell Teresa the background story. The girl had been an average student, and it is possible that she had felt the need to defend her grades by blaming the school. So she had told her mother that so much food was provided at JAMS that everyone just ate, watched movies, and danced. In addition, the students could wake up and go to bed whenever they wanted to. As if all that weren't distressing enough, her mother had been horrified that no corporal punishment was used at JAMS.

Instead of talking with Teresa, the mother had promptly pulled out her daughter and enrolled her in a school which rarely had graduates qualify for a university. Teresa was flabbergasted when she learned that the girl had been removed in part because of advantages offered at JAMS! She would have understood if the mother had chosen to withdraw her child because the school could not give her a strong preparation to succeed in the arts. That would have been a legitimate complaint about the newly-created institution.

As it was, Teresa would not be surprised if the mother tried to re-enroll her daughter at JAMS. But since she had not investigated the stories she had heard, she would be out of luck the next time.

The second story relates to the finances of the new school. Certainly, paying teachers' salaries is a top priority, and money from scholarships is set aside for that purpose. Then money paid by parents who struggle to meet the fees goes towards food and other expenses. This is why it is so important for the school to become as self-sustaining as possible by growing its own food and baking bread.

At times, Andrew and Teresa were advancing one or two months' pay to cover expenses. But it takes time for a school to grow to capacity. A new grade level was added each of the first four years. So more money came in each year. In addition, gradually the school moved past the heavy start-up costs that went to buying solar panels, hauling water, etc. All of this meant that teachers would be given raises during the fourth year.

Unfortunately, the English teacher, Betty, turned in her resignation before she could learn about the raise. She was offered 5000 shillings per month (approximately $60) more by another school, and that had convinced her to leave JAMS. This decision caught Teresa totally by surprise for a couple of reasons. The school had just purchased a set of French books since Betty had offered to teach French in addition to English. Further, Betty was a single mother, and she had expressed happiness that finally her daughter could be with her in the newly-completed teachers' residence. If only Betty had told Teresa that she was concerned about her salary! She would have received more than a penny for her thoughts.

"If You Steal From That School, You'll be Dead!"

Building a school in a region plagued by poverty poses some special challenges – particularly when essential items begin to disappear.

William was a young man who appeared to be a very dedicated casual laborer. Four days a week he tended the vegetable gardens, and one night he served as a watchman. This went well for a while, but soon Hesbon realized that the school was missing a sizable amount of timber – enough to build a whole house! Suspecting that William was working with some of the locals, he contacted the police. They paid a visit to a woman whose house was being constructed. She insisted that she had obtained the lumber from someone other than William. So the police compared the timber being used in her house with the timber at JAMS – it was a match. Realizing that this would seriously jeopardize her building project, the woman bribed the authorities, and that was the end of the problem – at least for her.

Teresa and Andrew learned that this was not the first time William had been guilty of thievery. In fact, he had been thrown out of his home because of stealing. But the school administrators took pity on him and told him that if he left, they would not press charges.

Not long after that, they discovered that William had been arrested and imprisoned for stealing a cell phone. Soon after he had been jailed, he got into a fight and died from his injuries. Teresa and Andrew were relieved that they had not been responsible for sending him to jail.

After William left, they hired Thomas. He was a likeable fellow, though rather lazy. Now Teresa and Andrew had bought a portable water pump for pumping water from the river. It turned out to be inefficient, so they purchased another one. This was at the beginning of the rainy season, so neither pump had been used for two months. Right before Teresa and Andrew were scheduled to return to the school, Hesbon inventoried the supplies, and discovered that both pumps were missing. So he called together all of the workers and explained the problem, saying "These people trusted us to watch the resources, but now the pumps are gone. Tell me by the end of the day where you think the pumps might be."

The workers suspected Thomas, and they started to pressure him to confess. He insisted that he knew nothing, and he walked away. His demeanor convinced the contractors that Thomas was indeed guilty, and they told Hesbon that if he would let them beat Thomas, they were sure they could get the pumps back.

Soon after Thomas walked away, Hesbon received a call from a villager who asked if he had lost something. He was told that if he went to a nearby sugar cane farm, he should count a certain number of rows, turn right, and walk a prescribed number of steps. Then he would find it. Hesbon followed the directions without any luck. So he kept searching inside the plantation, and soon he found one of the pumps.

Shortly after that, he received another call from the same villager, who told him where to find the second pump. Now he had retrieved both of the pumps, but he did not tell anyone at JAMS that they were found.

About that time, Thomas came to Hesbon, saying, "If you let me check, I think I can find them." Hesbon let him try, but of course he could not locate the pumps where he had hidden them. In the meantime, villagers saw him searching. Realizing that he was the guilty party, they were upset with him, and they informed him that the pumps had been found. That was the last time Hesbon saw Thomas. But the story has it that Thomas decided to disappear for a while with a friend (named Nelson Mendala!) who had been trying to find a buyer for the pumps.

The next time that Andrew and Teresa went to the local village, they were greeted with sympathetic people who insisted that they were furious with the scoundrels, and if Thomas or Nelson dared to come back, they would be dead. Not long after that, word reached the villagers that Nelson, who might have been HIV positive, had indeed died. This was enough to convince the superstitious people that, "If you steal from that school, you're dead!"

The Joys of Running Water

When Teresa and Andrew are at the school, they use their own pickup truck to haul food, water, and other supplies. But no one else knows how to drive it, so they leave it with Teresa's aunt. Every other week, she would bring items to the school, and once a month before the chicken coop was completed, she delivered a supply of eggs.

And of course, the school has a tractor to get anything which is needed urgently.

Transportation is essential, so the school purchased a new tractor, and they became convinced that this was one of the best decisions they made. Having their own functioning tractor saved a lot of money, the tractor moved easily on the rough ground, and best of all, there were three people at the school who could drive it. Parts for the tractor are purchased in the U.S. where they are cheaper. Since Andrew is an engineer, he can easily fix it.

Before they had running water, it was essential that the school own a 6000-liter water tank on wheels which attached to the tractor. In this way, water was carried from the river. During the dry season, a sugar cane factory nearby would give water freely to anyone with their own means of transportation. The factory pumped and purified its water, but since the JAMS tank also transported water from the river, the school still needed to treat any drinking and cooking water brought in the tank.

In addition to water carried in the tank, the school collected rain water funneled from roofs into six 20,000-liter tanks stored underground. Because of the tractor and the storage tanks, girls at the school did not need to spend time fetching water from the river, which would be a standard task if they were at home. (Other tasks which would consume their time at home would be collecting firewood, cooking for siblings, washing, and cleaning.)

Teresa was telling this story two weeks before she was about to head back to the school in mid-December, 2013. She noted that solar panels and water pipes had already been installed, and soon – after three years - the school would have running water pumped from a borehole. The borehole was drilled thanks to Larry Barnett of Barrington Rotary Club. He had climbed Mt. Kilimanjaro to raise money for the borehole.

Although Teresa was eagerly anticipating this development, she recognized that it would bring its own problems. Teresa recalled one time when the water tank pulled by the tractor was connected with a pump leading to pipes permitting the girls to take a shower in their dormitory. She had cautioned the girls to use the water sparingly. But for many of them, it was the first shower they had ever taken, and the supply of water – intended to last for two weeks - was pumped dry after 15 minutes. The girls had been so delighted with the water that they had not turned off the taps. Invoking natural consequences, Teresa told them that the school could not provide pumped water for two more weeks.

So Teresa knew that the girls would need to develop a habit of turning off faucets. In addition, during the rainy season, Andrew needed to solve the problem of how to divert water before it filled the septic tank.

In December, 2013, a water pump was installed, following a series of challenges – beginning with a 3 am trip to the main road for Andrew, who needed to wait for supplies that workers had forgotten to bring. It took four days to install the pump, partly because the project involved building a small house and installing eight very large solar panels on the roof. Having the panels meant that the pump would work even if there were only a few rays of sun during the day, which is a major concern during the rainy season.

It pumped 15,000 liters an hour, which sounds like a lot. Nevertheless, as predicted, the water ran out. The students were so thrilled with the running water that they delighted in simply letting the water flow over them. They enjoyed taking two showers a day. Teresa and Andrew decided not to say anything, but to wait for the novelty to wear off. When the girls realized that they could depend on running water, there would be fewer and shorter showers.

Déjà Vu All Over Again

In summer of 2014, Teresa experienced déjà vu in the worst possible sense when again she detected a laissez-faire attitude among the teachers. This time, two undergraduate interns accompanied her – Janet, an architectural student from Northeastern University in Boston, and Marguerite, a communications student from NIU. Marguerite made friends with the staff, and got to know them, while Janet visited their classes and observed their instruction. Janet quickly realized that teachers were routinely 20 minutes late to class – some of them were casually taking tea in the dining room. Even teachers who knew they would be observed would arrive significantly late to class, if they showed up at all.

To try to get a better handle on the problem, Teresa visited a neighboring school, asking "What do you do about teacher absenteeism?" She learned that they asked class prefects (students who were leaders) to keep records documenting when the teacher arrived and left. This proved to be a real eye-opener. All of the teachers were arriving late to class; the English teacher missed 10 classes in two weeks, and even the headmaster missed 9! It was clear that part of the problem was caused by having insufficient time to transition between classes, but that couldn't explain the whole situation.

So Teresa began attending some of the classes and talking with the teachers. She discovered that some of the teachers did not seem to think that their absences caused a problem, since they asked the students to meet with them during "prep" hours from 7 until 9 pm. Teresa tried to explain that the students were supposed to be doing homework during the evening hours. So when a math teacher met with them at night, that meant the girls could not use that time to complete their homework for another class.

She was appalled when she also discovered that some of the teachers were being unfair in their grading practices. On one exam, the religion teacher had asked why female genital mutilation was practiced. But she was not giving credit if a student replied with a "common sense" answer - that the practice would prevent women from enjoying sex.

The same teacher also taught geography. Typically, her students had arrived with grades of "B," yet the average test score in her class was a "D." Since the content was cumulative, students in form 3 would be tested on information from the first two years. Teresa speculated that at the current rate, the students would be receiving "F-" by the fourth year. It turned out that the teacher had been administering the form 4 test to second year students. She insisted that getting a harder exam would somehow motivate the students to work harder. Teresa had already discovered that common sense did not appear to be a strong suit of that teacher, so she tried to explain the illogic of using tests that did not relate to the material studied. She also noted that geography was an elective subject in forms three and four, but the students were so discouraged that none of them would choose to continue studying with that teacher. One week later, after receiving a test based on the material studied, "miraculously" the students' grades went from "D's" to "A's."

At the same time, the English teacher was awarding grades without giving feedback. For instance, one paper was given only 12 out of 20 points. While there were a couple of very minor problems, it was not at all evident why the essay had been graded so low. When asked to explain her grading, the teacher said simply, "It's just not good." Janet had attended a highly selective high school in the Midwest, yet she was clearly upset when she told Teresa that she would have failed the class by that teacher's standards.

So Teresa told the teacher that her grading practices were not helping the students, and she asked to see the rubric which was being used. The teacher replied, "I am grading based on my experience." When NIU English professor Diana saw the girls' work, she exclaimed that even some college students did not write as well as some JAMS students! Viewing the papers through her educated eyes, Diana frequently would have awarded the students 4 or 5 additional points. In addition, when the girls were tested using exams from another school, they routinely did better. So Teresa informed the teacher that many of the students were attending only because they had received scholarships, but their financial support depended on their performance. She added, "I don't mind if they are failing because they are doing badly, but you need to be doing your job!"

This prompted Teresa to examine the credentials of this teacher, who had been hired by the headmaster. The math did not add up. The woman claimed that she was 21. And yet, most people complete high school when they are 17, it takes them 4-5 years to finish college, and the woman reported that she had completed two years of teaching prior to coming to JAMS. It appeared she had lied.

Now Marguerite had been sitting in the staff room with the teachers, and had heard them complain about what a "dictator" Teresa seemed to be. But they had reassured themselves that as soon as she returned to the US, they could resume their preferred practices. Teresa sat down with them, saying, "You have a moral responsibility to this school. You are being paid, housed, and fed. All you need to do is to teach. If you don't do that, I have no reason to feed and house you. The only reason you are here is because of the students."

At the same time, Teresa was realizing that the problem seemed to go beyond individual teachers. She knew that for the most part, the teachers were talented. But they did not seem motivated to act responsibly. So she began zeroing in on the headmaster, who had been hired by the Teacher Service Commission. It turned out that he had accepted a second job with the Teacher Service Commission, and he was waiting to tell Teresa after the graduation ceremony. But for all practical purposes he had already "checked out," and the teachers knew that he had essentially left JAMS.

So Teresa realized that she needed to advertise for new staff members. She found that running an ad on a radio would cost 20,000 shillings ($250) for two weeks. Now that JAMS had adequate housing, running water, and electricity, the perks of working there were much more attractive. Indeed, it did not take long to hear from job applicants, and when she interviewed them, they appeared to be very good candidates.

For instance, Victor had experience teaching English in private schools in Nairobi, but those schools could not pay him enough to support his wife and two children. When Teresa told him that JAMS could provide two-room duplexes, food, and 18,000 shillings per month, he was amazed. Most private schools do not pay more than 10,000. (as opposed to public school Board of Governors, which pay only 3-4,000). In addition, Victor had leadership qualities which made him an attractive candidate for headmaster.

At the same time, there were some conscientious teachers at JAMS, and Benard was one of them. He was a very competent agriculture/biology teacher. Teresa decided to ask Victor and Benard to split the administrative duties and also to teach half time. Each of them would be paid 22,000 shillings.

Another applicant contacted Teresa from his school in Nakuru, which is an epicenter of tribal conflicts in Kenya. He was so eager to come that he wanted to begin immediately. However, once he arrived at

JAMS, he realized that he was not cut out for rural living – he could not conceive of a daily, long uphill walk, and he recommended a colleague. Similarly, this candidate was so excited about the prospect of coming to the school that he called Teresa every day to make sure that the position was still open. She promised that she would not offer the job to anyone until he had been interviewed.

Of course, some of the staff remembered that Teresa had not hesitated to fire all of the educators during the first year of the school. So when the teachers recognized that Teresa was serious about looking for new staff members, some decided to find out if they could do more to meet her expectations. She talked with them about their schedules. Following their evening classes, some of the teachers had expected the dining room to serve them their dinner. Teresa explained that the kitchen was closed at 7 pm because the cooks were expected to set up for breakfast beginning at 5 am the next morning. The headmaster urged the teachers to cook their own dinners in their apartments. But if they arrived at the dining room before 7, they would be fed. Some of the teachers simply needed to renew the commitment to meet their classes during the scheduled class time and to respect the fixed meal times. By the end of the summer, 2014, the school had 9 well-qualified, motivated teachers, including 3 women.

Beyond the Students: Effects of the School on Visitors

Whose lives have been affected by the school? The list extends well beyond the students who attend JAMS. Teresa remarked on how interns Marguerite and Janet grew from the experience of visiting the school.

Marguerite had visited the school six years earlier, while it was being built. At that time, she had been 16, and she had struggled with understanding the students' accents. As an upper middle class American teen, she had been amazed that students at the school did not have access to a swimming pool! But in 2014 she felt much more comfortable, so right from the start she interacted with the girls and the teachers. As a communications major, she was prepared to videotape her experiences. One thing that did surprise her on this trip was her discovery that the students at JAMS did not know anything about famous American presidents! Teresa challenged her, by asking, "How much do _you_ know about Jomo Kenyatta?"

Deflecting the question, Marguerite answered, "But they don't even know about slavery!" Teresa assured her that they really knew a lot about slavery, but perhaps the students could not understand Marguerite's accent. So this intern discovered that she needed to work on her communications skills.

When Marguerite and Janet shared a room, they reminded Teresa of the "odd couple." While Marguerite was easy-going and casual, Janet was more cautious. Of course, this was her first visit. So initially she was content simply to observe and to help with teacher evaluation. Being detached was an asset in her role as an evaluator, though she did regret not being invited to eat with the teachers. As an architecture student, Janet occupied herself by designing the school's science lab. And she read – constantly! This proved to be contagious, and Marguerite began reading for pleasure so that the girls could share what they were reading.

One might expect that young adults from the States would have their horizons expanded simply by coming to JAMS. But there are other ways in which visitors have grown. Making the trek to rural Kenya is one way to cut off ties with the outside world. This proved to be a crucial step towards reconnecting one mother-daughter pair. The father had left the family just before the girl was due to enter a residential high school. The mother and daughter had dealt with the loss independently, and they had drifted apart. Meeting a number of JAMS students who were orphans was an epiphany to the girl. She was surprised to see how well-adjusted and happy they seemed to be. She confided in Teresa, "I'm not going to get so stressed. I'm done expecting answers to everything. I'll wait and be patient." Coming to Africa permitted the mother and daughter to relate on a whole new level and to speak honestly with each other. The effect on their relationship was profound, and months later, just thinking about the experience still brought tears to the mother's eyes.

Wendy

The story of Wendy is another example of how the school has impacted lives beyond the students and teachers. One day in December, when a number of local people were working to prepare land for building a dairy at the school, Wendy sought out Teresa, saying, "Mama, can you give me some work?"

Teresa told her that a group of people were already working, why didn't she join them? The woman responded that she was new to the area, and she did not know anyone in the local tribe. So Teresa asked, "Where do you live?" Wendy pointed to a tiny mud hut nearby. It was no larger than 8 feet by 8 feet. This prompted Teresa to ask, "Where is your husband?" (In other words, why isn't he taking care of you?) The woman replied that her husband was very old, and she was his second wife, so by the time she came along, he had neither strength nor money.

So Teresa thought a minute and realized that she needed someone to level the ground around the fish ponds and plant vegetables there. Wendy beamed, "I've done that all my life. I'm very good at it."

Later, Teresa returned to the site, and was impressed at how meticulous the woman's work was, not to mention that she had accomplished "ten times as much" as the men who were hired. So Teresa found more work for Wendy.

At the same time, Andrew had been installing solar panels, and a number of cardboard boxes were stacked by a wall. Wendy asked him if she could have the boxes. He asked her what she would do with them, and she was evasive, "Don't worry, they'll be put to good use." Now the school has a rule that they do not usually allow people to cart trash away. This policy was created when Andrew and Teresa discovered that some people did not seem to be able to distinguish between items that were essential to the school, as opposed to junk. But this time Andrew made an exception. "You can take it, but we don't usually allow it. Later, Andrew and Teresa learned that the woman had used the cardboard for a makeshift bed. And she appreciated that it was so comfortable.

One of Teresa's goals has always been to give employment to women. But most of the construction jobs at JAMS have involved hard labor, so she had turned to men. This was problematic, since she had learned that "three fourths of them are so lazy." When I asked Andrew for perhaps a more objective perspective, he nodded sadly in agreement.

Because of the woman's work ethic, Teresa announced to Hesbon that the school was going to hire Wendy, and she would be paid 4000 shillings a month. Hesbon protested, "You can't give so much money to her!"

Teresa asked, "What would a man be paid?"

Hesbon replied, "4000 shillings."

So Teresa insisted that Wendy must be paid just as much.

When Wendy learned about her salary, she was overjoyed. She said that at most she had only expected 2000 shillings.

And she had some great ideas for the school. Once she asked to borrow Teresa's phone so that she could call her sister. She asked her to bring seeds for a drought-resistant kale which would thrive well at JAMS.

Now Wendy thought nothing about carrying water uphill in heavy buckets balanced on her head. But when Andrew and Teresa saw that, they asked the plumber to cut into the water line leading to their house and install a faucet closer to the vegetables.

Since then, Wendy has proven herself extremely trustworthy. Frequently she donates chickens to the school, and she has been promoted so that part of her job involves working in the JAMS kitchen. Teresa and Andrew need to be very careful about who has access to that part of the school, knowing how much damage could be caused by someone who poisons the food supply.

Even Hesbon has discovered how much he relies on Wendy's help. He has admitted, "You can't believe how much this lady is doing!"

Wendy describes her relationship with JAMS by quoting a Kenyan saying, "It's not the child you bare who will help you, but someone else's child will."

Benta

Benta is another Kenyan whose life has been transformed by working at JAMS. In Kenya, the woman who marries the oldest son in a family is destined to become the matriarch. So, even though Benta is much younger than Teresa, she is known as "Auntie" in Teresa's extended family. In addition, marriage is forever in Kenya, a country which has no word for divorce. So long after her relationship with Teresa's brother deteriorated, "Auntie" still oversees the farm which Jane Adeny had lovingly nurtured.

Teresa had recognized that Benta was very bright, but her parents could not afford to pay for her secondary education. Soon after Benta had married Teresa's brother, Teresa offered to finance her education. But it appeared that the young woman was more interested in trying to start a family.

Years later, Teresa's brother had died, and with financial help from Teresa, Benta was trying to manage the farm while raising four children. Throughout the time that JAMS was being built, Teresa would commute back and forth to her family's farm, where she would collapse with exhaustion while "Auntie" cooked and cleaned.

When it came time to open the school, Benta packed up pots, pans, and cooking sticks to set up the kitchen at JAMS. She spent two days cleaning the site, and then she became the school's cook. Teresa and Andrew have vowed that Benta will be on the school's payroll as long as they are alive. Benta still commutes daily between JAMS and the family farm – walking three miles to a bus, then another 1 ½ miles (including

400 feet uphill) from the bus stop to the school. She has hired a caretaker to watch over the family farm, and his family stays with her children during the day.

With the money from her job, she has purchased a water tank for the farm, and the villagers have grown to see Benta as being worthy of their respect. They even come to her for advice. She has the power to share water and maize. Without a doubt, she is a very good person, extremely honest, and a hard worker. In this way, she has transformed from a dependent beggar to someone who is independent and a contributing member of society.

In turn, Benta has a lot of respect for the teachers at JAMS. One day, soon after the school opened, Teresa looked outside her window. It was raining outside, yet there was Benta, picking her way over the rough terrain, balancing on her head a basin filled with food and covered with another basin. In her hand, she was carrying a pot of hot tea. Teresa rushed outside, asking what was happening. Benta replied, "If you don't get food to the teachers on time, they'll be mad." When she investigated further, Teresa discovered that the headteacher had not bothered to tell Benta not to bring a certain type of beans, so adding insult to injury, some of the food she had carefully balanced was not even eaten. Teresa was furious, asking "Why can't you come to the dining room to eat?" The teachers and the headmaster protested that they could not possibly eat with the students. So Teresa ordered that there would be no food for adults outside of the dining room.

An Inauguration / Commencement to Remember

The first students began attending JAMS in January of 2011. So they were in form 4 in 2014, and they were anticipating taking the high stakes final examinations in the fall of that year. Of course, usually graduation would follow the exams. However, Teresa decided to schedule the commencement in June, 2014, so that Diana, the President of the school's Board of Directors, could be present. This occasion would be full of pomp and circumstance, and it seemed like an ideal time to mark the official inauguration of the school. That event would require the presence of a priest to consecrate the school.

Now one of Teresa's aunts was married to the brother of the Arch Bishop. It so happened that Teresa ran into the clergy man at a funeral, so she took the opportunity to invite him to bless the school at its inauguration. The Arch Bishop exclaimed, "Do you mean it is a REAL school?!" When Teresa assured him that it was, he promised, "Just tell me the date and time, and I will come. But you will also need to invite a local priest to assist me in the ceremony."

So Teresa made sure that formal letters were drafted to invite these dignitaries. In addition, the students began writing letters inviting family members. Of course, a number of the girls are orphaned, so Teresa estimated that at most there would be approximately 200 guests. But when she shared this number with the students, they convinced her that she should expect a minimum of 600 guests, since they knew of many people who were curious and wanted to come see the school. In fact, the teachers thought that she might need to be prepared for 1000 visitors.

And of course, all of the guests needed to be fed. So the school purchased a cow to slaughter, and they made plans to kill one sheep, two goats, and 10 chickens. Teresa and one of her interns spent two solid days baking 300 loaves of bread. In addition, they would need to make sure there was sufficient water on hand. One of the most challenging needs would be building sufficient toilets for the huge crowd. That task was finally completed just in time – the day before the big event.

It occurred to Teresa that it had been a long time since she had heard from the Arch Bishop and the priest, so she decided to contact them several days before the ceremony. Still, she heard nothing until the day before the inauguration, when the priest informed her that he could not come since his brother had died recently. At 8 pm that evening – the night before the ceremony - the Arch Bishop's people called to confirm that he was coming. And oh, by the way, the school would need to provide a choir for the event.

The next day, at 6 am, people from the priest's church called with a list of additional requirements: the school needed to provide a table with a white tablecloth, flowers, a special chair, and even a separate toilet facility just for the Arch Bishop. Somehow, everything was ready by 10 am, when the ceremony was scheduled to begin. White sheets had been spread on the tables, 300 plates were stacked, every one of Teresa's nieces and nephews were on hand to serve food and wash dishes, and 700 guests were waiting expectantly. But the Arch Bishop was nowhere to be seen.

Four hours later, at 2 pm, the Arch Bishop arrived, along with the Bishop, and each was accompanied by his own retinue. So of course, now the school needed to make sure that there were two special chairs. In addition, a tree was to be planted in honor of the Arch Bishop, so now of course they needed to find an additional tree to plant for the

Bishop. Later, Teresa reflected that if she were ever to repeat the experience, she herself would say the prayer.

But still the ceremony could not commence. First the prelates needed to bless every inch of the buildings, including the toilets. Meanwhile, Teresa began serving food to the visitors who had waited so patiently.

Finally, at 4 pm, the Bishop and Arch Bishop were ready for the Graduation/ Inauguration.

By 6 pm, the ceremony was done, and every guest had been fed. Afterwards, Teresa noted ironically that comments she heard focused almost exclusively on the hospitality offered by the school – not on the excessive delay. People were impressed that they could eat as much as they wanted, that nice plates had been provided, and that there was enough water and plenty of toilets. In fact, the visitors remarked that the students did not look poor at all. Surely they had been misled - this was really a school for the rich. This was the talk of the neighboring communities for a long time following the big event.

Samburu Girls

Shortly after the graduation ceremony, Teresa learned about the plight of Samburu girls. The Samburu people, who are closely related to the Maasai, form a nomadic tribe in northeastern Kenya. Tribal customs defy the country's laws which prohibit female genital mutilation (fgm) and the forced marriage of young girls. Girls are viewed as a burden, so even some who are as young as 9 years old are circumcised and sold into marriage. In return, their family receives cows. The culture actively practices polygamy, and many families seek to sell their young daughters into marriage with wealthy older men who can afford to pay more cows.

The Samburu Girls' Foundation (SGF) was created by a young woman named Josephine Kulea. She is able to determine when a girl is about to be forced into fgm and marriage. With the support of the government, Josephine rescues these children and helps them enter a school. The Samburu community has made it clear that if these girls should return, they would face either marriage or death.

For a while, Josephine had worked out a partnership with a secondary school close to the tribe. But then she discovered that the conditions at that school were deplorable – not much better than a prison, and the Samburu girls were being treated as outcasts. Clearly, the girls did not want to be there, and the school admitted that they could not handle them. The mother of an SGF board member knew Teresa and recommended that girls who were old enough for secondary school be admitted to JAMS. Teresa agreed, so SGF piled 12 girls, ages 13 to 17, into a minivan and drove straight through, for 14 hours, from northeastern Kenya to the school in the far western part of the country.

Fortunately, their ages permitted them to be fairly evenly distributed across the first three forms of the school, and class sizes at JAMS now ranged around 20. Furthermore, the Samburu girls were highly motivated to learn. However, they had only attended school sporadically, so they arrived with weak educational backgrounds. Teresa arranged with other girls to tutor them to try to make up for deficiencies. While the Samburu Foundation could help with the girls' fees, they had already paid the other school for the fall semester of 2014, and that money could not be returned. So JAMS provided clothing, basic supplies, food, housing, and education for the girls, but would not begin receiving money until 2015. But how exciting it would be if Samburu students perform well on the national exams!

Final Exams and Life After JAMS

Girls who score at least a "C+" on the national exams can apply to public universities in Kenya. But if they earn a "B" or higher, they can receive a government subsidy. Subsidies are awarded on a quota system without regard to socioeconomic status. Since more boys qualify, they must score at least a "B+" to access this subsidy. Some years, when fewer girls earn qualifying grades, subsidies are awarded to girls who score "B-."

Without a government subsidy, public universities cost between $800 and $1000 per semester in tuition. Government subsidies cover both tuition and boarding for those who qualify. This money is considered a loan, so ultimately college graduates need to pay it back.

Clearly, these are high stakes tests, and Teresa characterizes the experience of preparing for the exams as "nightmarish." One reason the tests are so difficult is that they include facts taught in all of the previous grades. This could be a problem for the girls at JAMS, since the teachers they had encountered in form 1 had not been very competent. Before the school could provide adequate housing, they did not get the highest quality teachers applying.

That was why, in December, 2013, creating housing for teachers was a high priority for Teresa and Andrew. Previously, they could only attract teachers who lived a half hour away. The school had a four-bedroom guesthouse which was shared by three male teachers, but they could not hire female teachers who lived any distance from the school. So Teresa and Andrew found themselves working nonstop to finish and furnish two units in one house. From dawn to dusk, Teresa painted walls while

Andrew pounded on the roof to anchor and connect solar panels.

But it was well worth their aching muscles. Before they returned to the US in January, 2014, they were able to hire three teachers, including two women. Now that the school had suitable housing, as well as running water and electricity, it was easy to attract good teachers. As soon as educators saw the accommodations, they said, "I'm in."

So in spring, 2014, the first girls admitted to the school were "working in overdrive" in form 4 to make up for lessons they had missed. Although their performance on the mock exams had placed them among the top 5 out of 28 high schools in the region, the JAMS girls had earned no higher than a "B," and it was rumored that students often did worse on the national test.

However, after the mock exam results were released, a lady approached Teresa, telling her that she worked for a publisher which created books by the people who write the exams. Not only do the books include sample questions and answers, but they help students learn how to take the tests. She warned Teresa that the national schools tend to purchase all of the books quickly, So Teresa spent 20,000 shillings to purchase two books for each subject. She knew that the teachers would feel entitled to the books, so she set a policy that the books were not to leave a classroom, and the teachers were not to touch them.

Typically, students in form 4 in Kenya do not sleep. Frequently, students were studying in classrooms from 3 am until 11 pm. Teresa would protest, saying, "Your brain cannot function when you are sleep deprived. You have to sleep from 10 until 5."

But the teachers replied, "You have to be kidding. This is form 4. Even if students are in bed, they are not likely to be able to get to sleep, and they are sure to find a way around the rules about hours."

Finally, Teresa realized she was fighting a losing battle. She decided, "Let them study. If that gives them confidence, it is OK."

Post Graduate Opportunities

For all practical purposes, form 4 is completed as soon as the students finish their national exams in November. Assuming that they score a "C+" or higher on the test, the earliest they could enter college would not be until the following August. This could be a problem, particularly for the girls who do not have strong family support. Unless a girl has a father or a member of her father's family who is able to provide for and protect her, she would be at risk. According to Kenyan social norms the goal of the mother's family is to find a suitable match for a young woman so that she could move out of the home as quickly as possible. In the meantime, she would be considered a candidate for rape. Rather than subjecting these graduates to this uncertain future, they were asked to work at JAMS for a year.

So Teresa invited three at-risk girls who had completed form 4 to stay until college would begin. Marie, Carol, and Abigail were selected because they had proven themselves to be responsible. But equally important, they did not have safe places to stay before they began college.

They were assigned a variety of tasks related to the school's cottage industries. One of their first tasks was to market the school's bread. They carried samples of the bread they were baking and gave taste tests to shopkeepers in the nearby town. When they returned, they proudly reported that three shops had contracted to buy their bread. So they baked 30 loaves, took them to town on market day, and returned after just 2 hours, announcing that they had sold out immediately.

Not only were they responsible for selling the bread but for maintaining exact records – keeping track of every loaf. Teresa told them, "No loaf goes unsold," even if the school buys it. Because of this accounting, they were able to tell the school that they were on track to having a profitable bread-making enterprise. In the previous two years, JAMS had earned 50,000 shillings from bread sales. But now in just one month the school had made 10,000, and they expected the business to expand. Sales are boosted by Andrew. When he journeys to teach at a university in Nairobi, he takes some loaves with him. Each loaf sells for five shillings more in the big city than it would in the local village.

In order to accommodate the increased bread sales, the school purchased a machine to help the dough rise. So they no longer needed to depend on the sun for that part of the process, and now the school can make bread any time of the day or night.

Most other schools provide bread only to the students who can afford to buy it. But of course Teresa does not want to operate that way in a school which is good enough for the richest but open to the poorest.

In addition to baking bread, the three graduates became very good at painting buildings. Their culture had taught them that painting was a man's job. But by example Teresa assured them that "women can do it even better." So in just three days, Carol, Marie and Abigail had completed the job of painting two houses for teachers.

Of course, they were paid for their work. In addition, they earned money from serving as matrons in the dorms and from managing the fish and chickens at the school. Their goal was to earn the equivalent of $1000 by January, 2016. That would be enough to pay for initial fees for university entry. Theoretically, the government has a college loan system, but it is very corrupt, so girls coming from poverty are not likely to receive loans. It is essential that students have the funds to pay for the first year's tuition and for a safe place to live.

Unfortunately, university options are becoming more limited for the girls because of security and accommodations. Two universities closed due to riots over corruption. The students at those institutions had rioted in protest over the lack of safe housing which had been blamed for the death of a coed.

Inviting these three girls to work at the school for the year has benefited the school in a variety of ways. As was mentioned, these graduates had been particularly responsible students who set good examples. For instance, Carol had always demonstrated leadership qualities, and she had taken the initiative to care for the fish ponds while she had been a student. Naturally, this became one of her tasks after she graduated. Teresa has assured the current students that "it takes a certain character" to be selected. So the students are motivated to become involved in the school's industries, in hopes that they might be invited to assume a "post graduate" position.

Having the help from these girls has been especially helpful to the school since the micro-grant programs have been delayed.

Amazing Results

"AMAZING RESULTS: We are so happy to announce that the first graduates of Jane Adeny Memorial School for Girls have performed extremely well on their national secondary school exams. JAMS came out as #3 out of 28 schools in our district, an impressive result for the first time our students have taken the KCSE exam!"

With these words, the Friends of JAMS website announced the performance of the first graduating class. As soon as they heard the results, some of the students ran straight to the local public school to share their joy. Educators at that school had helped JAMS, but had always held a somewhat condescending attitude toward the startup. Students at new schools usually score no better than a "C" on the exams. It turned out the neighboring school had improved their showing on the test, but they had not done as well as the JAMS students.

Their principal remarked, "I have teachers with Master's but none of their students scored "A's" in the subject areas. How did you get good grades?"

Teresa's response was, "I didn't invest in teachers. I invested in the students." It should be noted that JAMS pays their teachers 18, 000 Kenyan shillings, while the other private school in the region pays 40,000. Indeed, the school had experienced a revolving door of teachers, but she had focused on building a good library and had told the girls that it was their responsibility to learn.

Teresa is convinced that one of the best investments she made was for the books which taught students how to take the national tests.

Having access to these resources gave the girls confidence, and their performance soared from an average of 5.7 on the mock exams to 7.8 on the national test. That type of increase is unheard of. Most schools are happy if their scores increase by .3 or .5. Teresa credits a history and religion teacher hired when the girls were in form 4 with helping to turn around their performance in that subject. She noted, "He worked so hard."

The mock tests had been useful in part because of feedback that the girls' performance was weakest in history and religious education. Apparently the person who had been teaching those subjects had not understood how to equip the students with critical thinking skills. Kenyan schools have a choice of either teaching about Christianity, Hinduism, or Islam. JAMS is located in a predominantly Christian area, so that is the focus at this school. But many of the Christian stories and symbols are similar to those of traditional African religions, and Teresa's intention is that whoever was hired to teach religion would note the parallels with respect.

The students' highest scores on the final exams were in geography/history, agriculture, and business. They also performed very well in physics. Some of the students, like Abigail, earned "A's" in math. This is unheard of in a girls' school, where typically math is not valued. Teresa was not surprised that students performed very poorly in languages, since the school did not have qualified English and Kiswahii instructors for the first three years.

Eleven (70%) of the 17 girls who took the tests received scores of "C+" or higher, which qualified them to enter universities. Since the lowest grade earned by JAMS students was "C-," the rest of the girls could enter a village polytechnic school. Those institutions focus on English and mathematics and prepare people for careers as healthcare workers, social workers, carpenters, early childhood teachers, teacher aids, etc.

One of the JAMS success stories concerns Sally, a girl who had come to the school at the age of 18. She had dismal primary school results – scoring only 200 points, while 250 was needed to enter most high schools. This probably was related to the fact that she had been extremely asthmatic, and her condition had been aggravated by malnutrition. Clearly, she had strengths. Teresa was impressed that Sally had not become pregnant when she had dropped out of school. But she had worked very hard and become very articulate in languages. When she scored "C+" on the final exam, she was ecstatic. It was phenomenal that someone scoring 200 on the primary tests would improve that much.

The chapters in this book have focused mainly on the stories of girls who had no other educational options available to them. These are the ones with whom Teresa developed the strongest relationships. However, it is worthwhile to note that some girls from relatively wealthy families have attended the school, and their parents have been grateful for the education received. One such girl had told her mother, "You can't hide in this school. In a bigger school, I'd be able to sleep in the dorm for two days!" Another scored "B-" on the national exams. Her father called the school to express his gratitude, saying that he had not expected her to earn even a "C," since she had scored poorly at the high school she attended before coming to JAMS. Apparently his daughter had been penalized in previous schools for thinking outside of the box. She assured him that she belonged at JAMS, saying "This is the only school for me. I can speak my mind and not get suspended!" Now she qualifies for any university in Kenya.

Certainly there is cause for much hope for the future. At the same time when form 4 students took the national exams, form 3 students took the mock exams. Three of JAMS's form 3 students earned straight

"A's," and seven of their students were in the top 10 students from the region. The performance of the first JAMS graduates is all the more impressive when one is reminded that most of the students had failed to qualify for national high schools; further, because of poverty, they had not been destined to access secondary school education. Teresa is convinced that the girls could have entered prestigious secondary schools if they had received a stronger education in primary school.

As a result of the tests, JAMS is now considered to be the best high school in the town, so Teresa hopes that more girls from wealthy families will be attracted to study at the school. This is important so that the school can afford to educate many students who cannot pay their fees. For every 20 students paying fees at JAMS, they can afford to educate five additional scholarship students. When the rotary club in Kenya can provide money for micro grants, Teresa anticipates that only 15 students will need full scholarships in the incoming class.

Plans for the Future

Doris received an "A-" on the national exams. She was supported at JAMS school by a church in DeKalb. Currently, Diana Swanson, a member of the church, is investigating whether Doris could be awarded a scholarship to study Humanities/Law at Northern Illinois University. This may be challenging for Doris. Abandoned by her extended family, Doris had come to JAMS as a "street smart" girl who survived by her wits. While at JAMS, Doris made a lot of progress in learning how to relate to others without resorting to aggression, but she still has further to go.

Carol earned a "B+" on the exams. She too would like to come to Northern Illinois to study. Her goal is to become a high school math or science teacher. She loves to teach. In fact, Teresa has observed that sometimes Carol does a better job than a more experienced teacher with explaining concepts to form 1 math students. In addition, she is willing to meet with the girls outside of class.

Abigail scored "A-" on the national tests, with "A's" in math and in science. She has been invited to apply to study engineering at Clemson University. At this point she is considering majoring in nuclear engineering. Truly this is amazing for a girl who had resigned herself to selling charcoal in a small village.

One of the luckiest students among the first graduates may be Marie, who earned a "B" on the exams and would like to study medicine. Kurt Thurmaier and his wife paid for her tuition throughout JAMS, and they have committed to paying for her tuition at a private college - $2000 per semester – as long as she keeps up her grades. Teresa mused that Marie is a very lucky young woman, and ironically part of her luck may be attributed to the fact that she is an orphan. If her parents had been alive, they would never have been able to afford the costs of a college.

This is one reason that Teresa encourages the students to appreciate the things that they have. One of their favorite show tunes is "My Favorite Things" from *The Sound of Music*. Focusing on their blessings has helped turn around the lives of many of the students at JAMS.

Initially the focus had been on doing whatever was necessary to start the school, and the motto was to create a school "good enough for the richest but open to the poorest." But as Teresa got to know the girls and their stories, her focus has shifted, and she is contemplating adopting a new motto, "Prosperity starts with an educated girl." Why? Because educating one girl pays dividends when it affects her children as well. The lives of many people will be impacted by this school. Just imagine the exponential effect when other school administrators in Kenyan discover the story of JAMS.

JAMS School

www.ingramcontent.com/pod-product-compliance
Lightning Source LLC
Chambersburg PA
CBHW021154020426
42331CB00003B/48